Desktop Outsourcing
Complete Self-Assessment Guide

C000060638

The guidance in this Self-Assessment is based on Desktop Outsourcing best practices and standards in business process architecture, design and quality management. The guidance is also based on the professional judgment of the individual collaborators listed in the Acknowledgments.

Table of Contents

About The Art of Service

The Art of Service, Business Process Architects since 2000, is dedicated to helping stakeholders achieve excellence.

Defining, designing, creating, and implementing a process to solve a stakeholders challenge or meet an objective is the most valuable role… In EVERY group, company, organization and department.

Unless you're talking a one-time, single-use project, there should be a process. Whether that process is managed and implemented by humans, AI, or a combination of the two, it needs to be designed by someone with a complex enough perspective to ask the right questions.

Someone capable of asking the right questions and step back and say, 'What are we really trying to accomplish here? And is there a different way to look at it?'

With The Art of Service's Standard Requirements Self-Assessments, we empower people who can do just that — whether their title is marketer, entrepreneur, manager, salesperson, consultant, Business Process Manager, executive assistant, IT Manager, CIO etc... —they are the people who rule the future. They are people who watch the process as it happens, and ask the right questions to make the process work better.

Contact us when you need any support with this Self-Assessment and any help with templates, blue-prints and examples of standard documents you might need:

http://theartofservice.com
service@theartofservice.com

Included Resources - how to access

Included with your purchase of the book is the Desktop

Outsourcing Self-Assessment Spreadsheet Dashboard which contains all questions and Self-Assessment areas and auto-generates insights, graphs, and project RACI planning - all with examples to get you started right away.

How? Simply send an email to
access@theartofservice.com
with this books' title in the subject to get the Desktop Outsourcing Self Assessment Tool right away.

You will receive the following contents with New and Updated specific criteria:

- The latest quick edition of the book in PDF

- The latest complete edition of the book in PDF, which criteria correspond to the criteria in...

- The Self-Assessment Excel Dashboard, and...

- Example pre-filled Self-Assessment Excel Dashboard to get familiar with results generation

- In-depth specific Checklists covering the topic

- Project management checklists and templates to assist with implementation

INCLUDES LIFETIME SELF ASSESSMENT UPDATES

Every self assessment comes with Lifetime Updates and Lifetime Free Updated Books. Lifetime Updates is an industry-first feature which allows you to receive verified self assessment updates, ensuring you always have the most accurate information at your fingertips.

Get it now- you will be glad you did - do it now, before you forget.

Send an email to **access@theartofservice.com** with this books' title in the subject to get the Desktop Outsourcing Self Assessment Tool right away.

Purpose of this Self-Assessment

This Self-Assessment has been developed to improve understanding of the requirements and elements of Desktop Outsourcing, based on best practices and standards in business process architecture, design and quality management.

It is designed to allow for a rapid Self-Assessment to determine how closely existing management practices and procedures correspond to the elements of the Self-Assessment.

The criteria of requirements and elements of Desktop Outsourcing have been rephrased in the format of a Self-Assessment questionnaire, with a seven-criterion scoring system, as explained in this document.

In this format, even with limited background knowledge of Desktop Outsourcing, a manager can quickly review existing operations to determine how they measure up to the standards. This in turn can serve as the starting point of a 'gap analysis' to identify management tools or system elements that might usefully be implemented in the organization to help improve overall performance.

How to use the Self-Assessment

On the following pages are a series of questions to identify to what extent your Desktop Outsourcing initiative is complete in comparison to the requirements set in standards.

To facilitate answering the questions, there is a space in front of each question to enter a score on a scale of '1' to '5'.

1 Strongly Disagree

2 Disagree

3 Neutral

4 Agree

5 Strongly Agree

Read the question and rate it with the following in front of mind:

'In my belief, the answer to this question is clearly defined'.

There are two ways in which you can choose to interpret this statement;
1. how aware are you that the answer to the question is clearly defined
2. for more in-depth analysis you can choose to gather evidence and confirm the answer to the question. This obviously will take more time, most Self-Assessment users opt for the first way to interpret the question and dig deeper later on based on the outcome of the overall Self-Assessment.

A score of '1' would mean that the answer is not clear at all, where a '5' would mean the answer is crystal clear and defined. Leave emtpy when the question is not applicable or you don't want to answer it, you can skip it without affecting your score. Write your score in the space provided.

After you have responded to all the appropriate statements in each section, compute your average score for that section, using the formula provided, and round to the nearest tenth. Then transfer to the corresponding spoke in the Desktop Outsourcing Scorecard on the second next page of the Self-Assessment.

Your completed Desktop Outsourcing Scorecard will give you a clear presentation of which Desktop Outsourcing areas need attention.

Desktop Outsourcing Scorecard Example

Example of how the finalized Scorecard can look like:

RECOGNIZE

SUSTAIN

DEFINE

CONTROL

MEASURE

IMPROVE

ANALYZE

Desktop Outsourcing Scorecard

Your Scores:

BEGINNING OF THE SELF-ASSESSMENT:

CRITERION #1: RECOGNIZE

INTENT: Be aware of the need for change. Recognize that there is an unfavorable variation, problem or symptom.

In my belief, the answer to this question is clearly defined:

5 Strongly Agree

4 Agree

3 Neutral

2 Disagree

1 Strongly Disagree

1. What problems are you facing and how do you consider Desktop Outsourcing will circumvent those obstacles?
<--- Score

2. Will new equipment/products be required to facilitate Desktop Outsourcing delivery, for example is new software needed?
<--- Score

3. As a sponsor, customer or management, how important is it to meet goals, objectives?
<--- Score

4. Are employees recognized or rewarded for performance that demonstrates the highest levels of integrity?
<--- Score

5. Is it clear when you think of the day ahead of you what activities and tasks you need to complete?
<--- Score

6. How many trainings, in total, are needed?
<--- Score

7. What are the stakeholder objectives to be achieved with Desktop Outsourcing?
<--- Score

8. How are you going to measure success?
<--- Score

9. Who else hopes to benefit from it?
<--- Score

10. For your Desktop Outsourcing project, identify and describe the business environment, is there more than one layer to the business environment?
<--- Score

11. Is it needed?
<--- Score

12. How does it fit into your organizational needs and

tasks?

<--- Score

13. What are the Desktop Outsourcing resources needed?

<--- Score

14. Are you dealing with any of the same issues today as yesterday? What can you do about this?

<--- Score

15. What is the problem or issue?

<--- Score

16. How can auditing be a preventative security measure?

<--- Score

17. Can management personnel recognize the monetary benefit of Desktop Outsourcing?

<--- Score

18. Who defines the rules in relation to any given issue?

<--- Score

19. How do you assess your Desktop Outsourcing workforce capability and capacity needs, including skills, competencies, and staffing levels?

<--- Score

20. Will Desktop Outsourcing deliverables need to be tested and, if so, by whom?

<--- Score

21. Consider your own Desktop Outsourcing

project, what types of organizational problems do you think might be causing or affecting your problem, based on the work done so far?
<--- Score

22. Where do you need to exercise leadership?
<--- Score

23. What do employees need in the short term?
<--- Score

24. How do you recognize an Desktop Outsourcing objection?
<--- Score

25. Are there recognized Desktop Outsourcing problems?
<--- Score

26. How do you identify the kinds of information that you will need?
<--- Score

27. When a Desktop Outsourcing manager recognizes a problem, what options are available?
<--- Score

28. Are there Desktop Outsourcing problems defined?
<--- Score

29. What are the timeframes required to resolve each of the issues/problems?
<--- Score

30. Which issues are too important to ignore?
<--- Score

31. Do you need different information or graphics?
<--- Score

32. What are your needs in relation to Desktop Outsourcing skills, labor, equipment, and markets?
<--- Score

33. What does Desktop Outsourcing success mean to the stakeholders?
<--- Score

34. Does the problem have ethical dimensions?
<--- Score

35. What are the minority interests and what amount of minority interests can be recognized?
<--- Score

36. Do you recognize Desktop Outsourcing achievements?
<--- Score

37. How are training requirements identified?
<--- Score

38. Why is this needed?
<--- Score

39. Why the need?
<--- Score

40. What do you need to start doing?
<--- Score

41. To what extent does each concerned units

management team recognize Desktop Outsourcing as an effective investment?
<--- Score

42. To what extent would your organization benefit from being recognized as a award recipient?
<--- Score

43. Are there any specific expectations or concerns about the Desktop Outsourcing team, Desktop Outsourcing itself?
<--- Score

44. What information do users need?
<--- Score

45. Did you miss any major Desktop Outsourcing issues?
<--- Score

46. Who needs what information?
<--- Score

47. Who are your key stakeholders who need to sign off?
<--- Score

48. Whom do you really need or want to serve?
<--- Score

49. Who should resolve the Desktop Outsourcing issues?
<--- Score

50. Are controls defined to recognize and contain

problems?

<--- Score

51. How are the Desktop Outsourcing's objectives aligned to the group's overall stakeholder strategy?

<--- Score

52. What training and capacity building actions are needed to implement proposed reforms?

<--- Score

53. What resources or support might you need?

<--- Score

54. What extra resources will you need?

<--- Score

55. Where is training needed?

<--- Score

56. Will it solve real problems?

<--- Score

57. How do you identify subcontractor relationships?

<--- Score

58. What would happen if Desktop Outsourcing weren't done?

<--- Score

59. What is the recognized need?

<--- Score

60. Which needs are not included or involved?

<--- Score

61. How do you recognize an objection?
<--- Score

62. What should be considered when identifying available resources, constraints, and deadlines?
<--- Score

63. What activities does the governance board need to consider?
<--- Score

64. What is the problem and/or vulnerability?
<--- Score

65. What Desktop Outsourcing events should you attend?
<--- Score

66. Are there regulatory / compliance issues?
<--- Score

67. Are losses recognized in a timely manner?
<--- Score

68. Have you identified your Desktop Outsourcing key performance indicators?
<--- Score

69. Is the quality assurance team identified?
<--- Score

70. How much are sponsors, customers, partners, stakeholders involved in Desktop Outsourcing? In other words, what are the risks, if Desktop Outsourcing does not deliver successfully?
<--- Score

71. What else needs to be measured?
<--- Score

72. What prevents you from making the changes you know will make you a more effective Desktop Outsourcing leader?
<--- Score

73. What needs to be done?
<--- Score

74. Are there any revenue recognition issues?
<--- Score

75. Think about the people you identified for your Desktop Outsourcing project and the project responsibilities you would assign to them, what kind of training do you think they would need to perform these responsibilities effectively?
<--- Score

76. What are the expected benefits of Desktop Outsourcing to the stakeholder?
<--- Score

77. Does your organization need more Desktop Outsourcing education?
<--- Score

78. Will a response program recognize when a crisis occurs and provide some level of response?
<--- Score

79. How do you take a forward-looking perspective in identifying Desktop Outsourcing research related to

market response and models?
<--- Score

80. What Desktop Outsourcing capabilities do you need?
<--- Score

81. What creative shifts do you need to take?
<--- Score

82. Do you have/need 24-hour access to key personnel?
<--- Score

83. Are employees recognized for desired behaviors?
<--- Score

84. Who needs to know?
<--- Score

85. What is the Desktop Outsourcing problem definition? What do you need to resolve?
<--- Score

86. What vendors make products that address the Desktop Outsourcing needs?
<--- Score

87. Is the need for organizational change recognized?
<--- Score

88. Do you know what you need to know about Desktop Outsourcing?
<--- Score

89. What Desktop Outsourcing problem should be solved?

<--- Score

90. What is the smallest subset of the problem you can usefully solve?

<--- Score

91. Are problem definition and motivation clearly presented?

<--- Score

92. Do you need to avoid or amend any Desktop Outsourcing activities?

<--- Score

93. What Desktop Outsourcing coordination do you need?

<--- Score

94. What situation(s) led to this Desktop Outsourcing Self Assessment?

<--- Score

95. What are the clients issues and concerns?

<--- Score

96. Are your goals realistic? Do you need to redefine your problem? Perhaps the problem has changed or maybe you have reached your goal and need to set a new one?

<--- Score

97. Who needs to know about Desktop Outsourcing?

<--- Score

98. Who needs budgets?
<--- Score

99. What is the extent or complexity of the Desktop Outsourcing problem?
<--- Score

100. What tools and technologies are needed for a custom Desktop Outsourcing project?
<--- Score

Add up total points for this section:
_ _ _ _ _ = Total points for this section

Divided by: _ _ _ _ _ _ (number of statements answered) = _ _ _ _ _ _ Average score for this section

Transfer your score to the Desktop Outsourcing Index at the beginning of the Self-Assessment.

CRITERION #2: DEFINE:

INTENT: Formulate the stakeholder problem. Define the problem, needs and objectives.

In my belief, the answer to this question is clearly defined:

5 Strongly Agree

4 Agree

3 Neutral

2 Disagree

1 Strongly Disagree

1. What would be the goal or target for a Desktop Outsourcing's improvement team?
<--- Score

2. What are the Roles and Responsibilities for each team member and its leadership? Where is this documented?
<--- Score

3. What is in the scope and what is not in scope?
<--- Score

4. Do you all define Desktop Outsourcing in the same way?
<--- Score

5. What Desktop Outsourcing requirements should be gathered?
<--- Score

6. What was the context?
<--- Score

7. Have the customer needs been translated into specific, measurable requirements? How?
<--- Score

8. Have all basic functions of Desktop Outsourcing been defined?
<--- Score

9. What information should you gather?
<--- Score

10. Are roles and responsibilities formally defined?
<--- Score

11. Is it clearly defined in and to your organization what you do?
<--- Score

12. Are the Desktop Outsourcing requirements complete?
<--- Score

13. What scope to assess?
<--- Score

14. How can the value of Desktop Outsourcing be defined?
<--- Score

15. What are the requirements for audit information?
<--- Score

16. How often are the team meetings?
<--- Score

17. Have all of the relationships been defined properly?
<--- Score

18. Are approval levels defined for contracts and supplements to contracts?
<--- Score

19. Is there a completed SIPOC representation, describing the Suppliers, Inputs, Process, Outputs, and Customers?
<--- Score

20. Are customer(s) identified and segmented according to their different needs and requirements?
<--- Score

21. Who is gathering information?
<--- Score

22. Who defines (or who defined) the rules and roles?

<--- Score

23. Has a high-level 'as is' process map been completed, verified and validated?
<--- Score

24. How do you catch Desktop Outsourcing definition inconsistencies?
<--- Score

25. Are required metrics defined, what are they?
<--- Score

26. Is there a clear Desktop Outsourcing case definition?
<--- Score

27. When is/was the Desktop Outsourcing start date?
<--- Score

28. Who approved the Desktop Outsourcing scope?
<--- Score

29. Why are you doing Desktop Outsourcing and what is the scope?
<--- Score

30. How would you define the culture at your organization, how susceptible is it to Desktop Outsourcing changes?
<--- Score

31. If substitutes have been appointed, have they been briefed on the Desktop Outsourcing goals and received regular communications as to the progress to date?

<--- Score

32. Are different versions of process maps needed to account for the different types of inputs?
<--- Score

33. Is Desktop Outsourcing currently on schedule according to the plan?
<--- Score

34. What information do you gather?
<--- Score

35. Is there regularly 100% attendance at the team meetings? If not, have appointed substitutes attended to preserve cross-functionality and full representation?
<--- Score

36. How would you define Desktop Outsourcing leadership?
<--- Score

37. Are accountability and ownership for Desktop Outsourcing clearly defined?
<--- Score

38. Is the Desktop Outsourcing scope complete and appropriately sized?
<--- Score

39. Have specific policy objectives been defined?
<--- Score

40. What key stakeholder process output measure(s) does Desktop Outsourcing leverage and how?

<--- Score

41. Has the improvement team collected the 'voice of the customer' (obtained feedback – qualitative and quantitative)?
<--- Score

42. What is the scope of the Desktop Outsourcing effort?
<--- Score

43. How do you hand over Desktop Outsourcing context?
<--- Score

44. Has/have the customer(s) been identified?
<--- Score

45. Is there a completed, verified, and validated high-level 'as is' (not 'should be' or 'could be') stakeholder process map?
<--- Score

46. Do the problem and goal statements meet the SMART criteria (specific, measurable, attainable, relevant, and time-bound)?
<--- Score

47. What is the context?
<--- Score

48. How do you gather the stories?
<--- Score

49. What are the boundaries of the scope? What is in bounds and what is not? What is the start point? What

is the stop point?
<--- Score

50. What is out of scope?
<--- Score

51. Is the team adequately staffed with the desired cross-functionality? If not, what additional resources are available to the team?
<--- Score

52. What is out-of-scope initially?
<--- Score

53. Where can you gather more information?
<--- Score

54. How do you think the partners involved in Desktop Outsourcing would have defined success?
<--- Score

55. How did the Desktop Outsourcing manager receive input to the development of a Desktop Outsourcing improvement plan and the estimated completion dates/times of each activity?
<--- Score

56. What are the tasks and definitions?
<--- Score

57. Will a Desktop Outsourcing production readiness review be required?
<--- Score

58. Is the Desktop Outsourcing scope manageable?
<--- Score

59. What is the definition of success?
<--- Score

60. What are the Desktop Outsourcing tasks and definitions?
<--- Score

61. How does the Desktop Outsourcing manager ensure against scope creep?
<--- Score

62. Has a project plan, Gantt chart, or similar been developed/completed?
<--- Score

63. Is the improvement team aware of the different versions of a process: what they think it is vs. what it actually is vs. what it should be vs. what it could be?
<--- Score

64. How do you keep key subject matter experts in the loop?
<--- Score

65. Is Desktop Outsourcing linked to key stakeholder goals and objectives?
<--- Score

66. Is the scope of Desktop Outsourcing defined?
<--- Score

67. Are there different segments of customers?
<--- Score

68. What are the record-keeping requirements of

Desktop Outsourcing activities?

<--- Score

69. What baselines are required to be defined and managed?

<--- Score

70. What specifically is the problem? Where does it occur? When does it occur? What is its extent?

<--- Score

71. Will team members regularly document their Desktop Outsourcing work?

<--- Score

72. How do you manage changes in Desktop Outsourcing requirements?

<--- Score

73. Is there a critical path to deliver Desktop Outsourcing results?

<--- Score

74. What sort of initial information to gather?

<--- Score

75. When are meeting minutes sent out? Who is on the distribution list?

<--- Score

76. Has a team charter been developed and communicated?

<--- Score

77. Has everyone on the team, including the team leaders, been properly trained?

<--- Score

78. What critical content must be communicated –
who, what, when, where, and how?
<--- Score

79. What are the rough order estimates on cost
savings/opportunities that Desktop Outsourcing
brings?
<--- Score

80. What Desktop Outsourcing services do you
require?
<--- Score

81. Is the team equipped with available and reliable
resources?
<--- Score

82. Are audit criteria, scope, frequency and methods
defined?
<--- Score

**83. How do you gather Desktop Outsourcing
requirements?**
<--- Score

84. What constraints exist that might impact the
team?
<--- Score

85. What gets examined?
<--- Score

**86. Has a Desktop Outsourcing requirement not
been met?**

<--- Score

87. Are task requirements clearly defined?
<--- Score

88. Has your scope been defined?
<--- Score

89. What are the Desktop Outsourcing use cases?
<--- Score

90. What are the compelling stakeholder reasons for embarking on Desktop Outsourcing?
<--- Score

91. The political context: who holds power?
<--- Score

92. Is Desktop Outsourcing required?
<--- Score

93. How was the 'as is' process map developed, reviewed, verified and validated?
<--- Score

94. Are resources adequate for the scope?
<--- Score

95. How have you defined all Desktop Outsourcing requirements first?
<--- Score

96. Is the work to date meeting requirements?
<--- Score

97. What is the scope of Desktop Outsourcing?

<--- Score

98. What is the worst case scenario?
<--- Score

99. Who is gathering Desktop Outsourcing information?
<--- Score

100. How will variation in the actual durations of each activity be dealt with to ensure that the expected Desktop Outsourcing results are met?
<--- Score

101. Do you have a Desktop Outsourcing success story or case study ready to tell and share?
<--- Score

102. Is data collected and displayed to better understand customer(s) critical needs and requirements.
<--- Score

103. Has the direction changed at all during the course of Desktop Outsourcing? If so, when did it change and why?
<--- Score

104. Is the current 'as is' process being followed? If not, what are the discrepancies?
<--- Score

105. What customer feedback methods were used to solicit their input?
<--- Score

106. Has the Desktop Outsourcing work been fairly and/or equitably divided and delegated among team members who are qualified and capable to perform the work? Has everyone contributed?
<--- Score

107. What is the definition of Desktop Outsourcing excellence?
<--- Score

108. What sources do you use to gather information for a Desktop Outsourcing study?
<--- Score

109. When is the estimated completion date?
<--- Score

110. Is there a Desktop Outsourcing management charter, including stakeholder case, problem and goal statements, scope, milestones, roles and responsibilities, communication plan?
<--- Score

111. What are (control) requirements for Desktop Outsourcing Information?
<--- Score

112. How will the Desktop Outsourcing team and the group measure complete success of Desktop Outsourcing?
<--- Score

113. Has anyone else (internal or external to the group) attempted to solve this problem or a similar one before? If so, what knowledge can be leveraged from these previous efforts?

<--- Score

114. Who are the Desktop Outsourcing improvement team members, including Management Leads and Coaches?
<--- Score

115. What is the scope?
<--- Score

116. How are consistent Desktop Outsourcing definitions important?
<--- Score

117. In what way can you redefine the criteria of choice clients have in your category in your favor?
<--- Score

118. How do you manage scope?
<--- Score

119. Is there any additional Desktop Outsourcing definition of success?
<--- Score

120. What are the dynamics of the communication plan?
<--- Score

121. How do you manage unclear Desktop Outsourcing requirements?
<--- Score

122. How is the team tracking and documenting its work?
<--- Score

123. What intelligence can you gather?
<--- Score

124. Is special Desktop Outsourcing user knowledge required?
<--- Score

125. What is in scope?
<--- Score

126. Does the team have regular meetings?
<--- Score

127. Does the scope remain the same?
<--- Score

128. What are the core elements of the Desktop Outsourcing business case?
<--- Score

129. What is a worst-case scenario for losses?
<--- Score

130. How and when will the baselines be defined?
<--- Score

131. How do you build the right business case?
<--- Score

132. Are all requirements met?
<--- Score

133. What is the scope of the Desktop Outsourcing work?
<--- Score

134. Are there any constraints known that bear on the ability to perform Desktop Outsourcing work? How is the team addressing them?
<--- Score

135. What system do you use for gathering Desktop Outsourcing information?
<--- Score

Add up total points for this section:
_ _ _ _ _ = Total points for this section

Divided by: _ _ _ _ _ _ (number of statements answered) = _ _ _ _ _ _
Average score for this section

Transfer your score to the Desktop Outsourcing Index at the beginning of the Self-Assessment.

CRITERION #3: MEASURE:

INTENT: Gather the correct data. Measure the current performance and evolution of the situation.

In my belief, the answer to this question is clearly defined:

5 Strongly Agree

4 Agree

3 Neutral

2 Disagree

1 Strongly Disagree

1. How do you verify the authenticity of the data and information used?
<--- Score

2. How will your organization measure success?
<--- Score

3. Are missed Desktop Outsourcing opportunities costing your organization money?

<--- Score

4. Are the Desktop Outsourcing benefits worth its costs?
<--- Score

5. How can a Desktop Outsourcing test verify your ideas or assumptions?
<--- Score

6. What could cause delays in the schedule?
<--- Score

7. What users will be impacted?
<--- Score

8. How will measures be used to manage and adapt?
<--- Score

9. Why do the measurements/indicators matter?
<--- Score

10. Was a business case (cost/benefit) developed?
<--- Score

11. When a disaster occurs, who gets priority?
<--- Score

12. Why do you expend time and effort to implement measurement, for whom?
<--- Score

13. The approach of traditional Desktop Outsourcing works for detail complexity but is focused on a systematic approach rather than an understanding of the nature of systems

themselves, what approach will permit your organization to deal with the kind of unpredictable emergent behaviors that dynamic complexity can introduce?
<--- Score

14. Do you effectively measure and reward individual and team performance?
<--- Score

15. Do the benefits outweigh the costs?
<--- Score

16. What would be a real cause for concern?
<--- Score

17. Will Desktop Outsourcing have an impact on current business continuity, disaster recovery processes and/or infrastructure?
<--- Score

18. Are there any easy-to-implement alternatives to Desktop Outsourcing? Sometimes other solutions are available that do not require the cost implications of a full-blown project?
<--- Score

19. Do you verify that corrective actions were taken?
<--- Score

20. How do you focus on what is right -not who is right?
<--- Score

21. How long to keep data and how to manage

retention costs?

<--- Score

22. What do you measure and why?

<--- Score

23. How do you measure efficient delivery of Desktop Outsourcing services?

<--- Score

24. Is the solution cost-effective?

<--- Score

25. How do you verify your resources?

<--- Score

26. How do you prevent mis-estimating cost?

<--- Score

27. How do you verify the Desktop Outsourcing requirements quality?

<--- Score

28. How do you measure variability?

<--- Score

29. What is your decision requirements diagram?

<--- Score

30. Do you have any cost Desktop Outsourcing limitation requirements?

<--- Score

31. What is the Desktop Outsourcing business impact?

<--- Score

32. Does a Desktop Outsourcing quantification method exist?

<--- Score

33. What are your key Desktop Outsourcing organizational performance measures, including key short and longer-term financial measures?

<--- Score

34. Are there measurements based on task performance?

<--- Score

35. What are the costs?

<--- Score

36. Are you able to realize any cost savings?

<--- Score

37. When should you bother with diagrams?

<--- Score

38. How can you measure Desktop Outsourcing in a systematic way?

<--- Score

39. Are actual costs in line with budgeted costs?

<--- Score

40. What methods are feasible and acceptable to estimate the impact of reforms?

<--- Score

41. Are indirect costs charged to the Desktop Outsourcing program?

<--- Score

42. Is the cost worth the Desktop Outsourcing effort ?
<--- Score

43. Are the units of measure consistent?
<--- Score

44. What causes innovation to fail or succeed in your organization?
<--- Score

45. What is the total fixed cost?
<--- Score

46. What are allowable costs?
<--- Score

47. Which costs should be taken into account?
<--- Score

48. What is your Desktop Outsourcing quality cost segregation study?
<--- Score

49. What does your operating model cost?
<--- Score

50. How are costs allocated?
<--- Score

51. What causes mismanagement?
<--- Score

52. Have you made assumptions about the shape of the future, particularly its impact on your customers and competitors?

<--- Score

53. How do you verify performance?

<--- Score

54. What measurements are possible, practicable and meaningful?

<--- Score

55. How do you quantify and qualify impacts?

<--- Score

56. How is performance measured?

<--- Score

57. Who pays the cost?

<--- Score

58. How can you reduce the costs of obtaining inputs?

<--- Score

59. What causes investor action?

<--- Score

60. What are the Desktop Outsourcing investment costs?

<--- Score

61. How much does it cost?

<--- Score

62. Are you taking your company in the direction of better and revenue or cheaper and cost?

<--- Score

63. Does the Desktop Outsourcing task fit the

client's priorities?
<--- Score

64. What drives O&M cost?
<--- Score

65. At what cost?
<--- Score

66. Who is involved in verifying compliance?
<--- Score

67. Does management have the right priorities among projects?
<--- Score

68. Is it possible to estimate the impact of unanticipated complexity such as wrong or failed assumptions, feedback, etcetera on proposed reforms?
<--- Score

69. Are there competing Desktop Outsourcing priorities?
<--- Score

70. How frequently do you track Desktop Outsourcing measures?
<--- Score

71. What does losing customers cost your organization?
<--- Score

72. Are the measurements objective?
<--- Score

73. What is measured? Why?

<--- Score

74. What causes extra work or rework?

<--- Score

75. How do you verify and develop ideas and innovations?

<--- Score

76. What are the costs of delaying Desktop Outsourcing action?

<--- Score

77. How can you measure the performance?

<--- Score

78. What are your customers expectations and measures?

<--- Score

79. What does verifying compliance entail?

<--- Score

80. How are you verifying it?

<--- Score

81. How do you aggregate measures across priorities?

<--- Score

82. What disadvantage does this cause for the user?

<--- Score

83. When are costs are incurred?

<--- Score

84. How do you measure success?
<--- Score

85. What would it cost to replace your technology?
<--- Score

86. What tests verify requirements?
<--- Score

87. What are the types and number of measures to use?
<--- Score

88. Who should receive measurement reports?
<--- Score

89. How is the value delivered by Desktop Outsourcing being measured?
<--- Score

90. What is the cost of rework?
<--- Score

91. Has a cost center been established?
<--- Score

92. What does a Test Case verify?
<--- Score

93. What is an unallowable cost?
<--- Score

94. What is the root cause(s) of the problem?
<--- Score

95. What are the costs of reform?
<--- Score

96. What evidence is there and what is measured?
<--- Score

97. What are your operating costs?
<--- Score

98. Where can you go to verify the info?
<--- Score

99. What are the current costs of the Desktop Outsourcing process?
<--- Score

100. How will effects be measured?
<--- Score

101. What are hidden Desktop Outsourcing quality costs?
<--- Score

102. What are your primary costs, revenues, assets?
<--- Score

103. How will costs be allocated?
<--- Score

104. Are you aware of what could cause a problem?
<--- Score

105. What details are required of the Desktop Outsourcing cost structure?
<--- Score

106. Is there an opportunity to verify requirements?
<--- Score

107. What are the operational costs after Desktop Outsourcing deployment?
<--- Score

108. How is progress measured?
<--- Score

109. What are the Desktop Outsourcing key cost drivers?
<--- Score

110. Why a Desktop Outsourcing focus?
<--- Score

111. How will you measure your Desktop Outsourcing effectiveness?
<--- Score

112. How do your measurements capture actionable Desktop Outsourcing information for use in exceeding your customers expectations and securing your customers engagement?
<--- Score

113. Which measures and indicators matter?
<--- Score

114. Do you have a flow diagram of what happens?
<--- Score

115. What can be used to verify compliance?
<--- Score

116. What are the strategic priorities for this year?
<--- Score

117. Do you have an issue in getting priority?
<--- Score

118. How do you verify and validate the Desktop Outsourcing data?
<--- Score

119. What relevant entities could be measured?
<--- Score

120. How do you measure lifecycle phases?
<--- Score

121. What do people want to verify?
<--- Score

122. How will you measure success?
<--- Score

123. How can you reduce costs?
<--- Score

124. What are the uncertainties surrounding estimates of impact?
<--- Score

125. How sensitive must the Desktop Outsourcing strategy be to cost?
<--- Score

126. What is the total cost related to deploying Desktop Outsourcing, including any consulting or

professional services?

<--- Score

127. How will success or failure be measured?

<--- Score

128. What happens if cost savings do not materialize?

<--- Score

129. How do you verify if Desktop Outsourcing is built right?

<--- Score

130. Among the Desktop Outsourcing product and service cost to be estimated, which is considered hardest to estimate?

<--- Score

131. What are you verifying?

<--- Score

132. Do you aggressively reward and promote the people who have the biggest impact on creating excellent Desktop Outsourcing services/products?

<--- Score

133. What potential environmental factors impact the Desktop Outsourcing effort?

<--- Score

134. How do you control the overall costs of your work processes?

<--- Score

135. What measurements are being captured?

<--- Score

136. What are the estimated costs of proposed changes?
<--- Score

137. How frequently do you verify your Desktop Outsourcing strategy?
<--- Score

138. Have design-to-cost goals been established?
<--- Score

139. Where is the cost?
<--- Score

Add up total points for this section:
_____ = Total points for this section

Divided by: _____ (number of statements answered) = _____
Average score for this section

Transfer your score to the Desktop Outsourcing Index at the beginning of the Self-Assessment.

CRITERION #4: ANALYZE:

INTENT: Analyze causes, assumptions
and hypotheses.

In my belief, the answer to this
question is clearly defined:

5 Strongly Agree

4 Agree

3 Neutral

2 Disagree

1 Strongly Disagree

1. How does the organization define, manage, and improve its Desktop Outsourcing processes?
<--- Score

2. Have any additional benefits been identified that will result from closing all or most of the gaps?
<--- Score

3. Do quality systems drive continuous improvement?

<--- Score

4. Think about some of the processes you undertake within your organization, which do you own?
<--- Score

5. How will the change process be managed?
<--- Score

6. Do staff qualifications match your project?
<--- Score

7. How can risk management be tied procedurally to process elements?
<--- Score

8. An organizationally feasible system request is one that considers the mission, goals and objectives of the organization, key questions are: is the Desktop Outsourcing solution request practical and will it solve a problem or take advantage of an opportunity to achieve company goals?
<--- Score

9. What does the data say about the performance of the stakeholder process?
<--- Score

10. What controls do you have in place to protect data?
<--- Score

11. What training and qualifications will you need?
<--- Score

12. Is there an established change management

process?
<--- Score

13. Do you understand your management processes today?
<--- Score

14. What tools were used to narrow the list of possible causes?
<--- Score

15. Who is involved in the management review process?
<--- Score

16. What are your Desktop Outsourcing processes?
<--- Score

17. Who gets your output?
<--- Score

18. When should a process be art not science?
<--- Score

19. Are your outputs consistent?
<--- Score

20. How is Desktop Outsourcing data gathered?
<--- Score

21. What successful thing are you doing today that may be blinding you to new growth opportunities?
<--- Score

22. What systems/processes must you excel at?
<--- Score

23. How is the way you as the leader think and process information affecting your organizational culture?
<--- Score

24. How do you use Desktop Outsourcing data and information to support organizational decision making and innovation?
<--- Score

25. What Desktop Outsourcing metrics are outputs of the process?
<--- Score

26. How has the Desktop Outsourcing data been gathered?
<--- Score

27. Is the suppliers process defined and controlled?
<--- Score

28. What are the revised rough estimates of the financial savings/opportunity for Desktop Outsourcing improvements?
<--- Score

29. How many input/output points does it require?
<--- Score

30. Is the Desktop Outsourcing process severely broken such that a re-design is necessary?
<--- Score

31. How do you implement and manage your work processes to ensure that they meet design requirements?

<--- Score

32. What resources go in to get the desired output?
<--- Score

33. What is the oversight process?
<--- Score

34. What is the output?
<--- Score

35. How is the data gathered?
<--- Score

36. Think about the functions involved in your Desktop Outsourcing project, what processes flow from these functions?
<--- Score

37. How do you measure the operational performance of your key work systems and processes, including productivity, cycle time, and other appropriate measures of process effectiveness, efficiency, and innovation?
<--- Score

38. How is the Desktop Outsourcing Value Stream Mapping managed?
<--- Score

39. What kind of crime could a potential new hire have committed that would not only not disqualify him/her from being hired by your organization, but would actually indicate that he/she might be a particularly good fit?
<--- Score

40. Where is Desktop Outsourcing data gathered?
<--- Score

41. What Desktop Outsourcing data will be collected?
<--- Score

42. What, related to, Desktop Outsourcing processes does your organization outsource?
<--- Score

43. Were Pareto charts (or similar) used to portray the 'heavy hitters' (or key sources of variation)?
<--- Score

44. Who will gather what data?
<--- Score

45. What qualifications and skills do you need?
<--- Score

46. Was a detailed process map created to amplify critical steps of the 'as is' stakeholder process?
<--- Score

47. What were the financial benefits resulting from any 'ground fruit or low-hanging fruit' (quick fixes)?
<--- Score

48. Has data output been validated?
<--- Score

49. How will the data be checked for quality?
<--- Score

50. What data do you need to collect?

<--- Score

51. What did the team gain from developing a sub-process map?
<--- Score

52. Are all staff in core Desktop Outsourcing subjects Highly Qualified?
<--- Score

53. What were the crucial 'moments of truth' on the process map?
<--- Score

54. Who is involved with workflow mapping?
<--- Score

55. Is there a strict change management process?
<--- Score

56. What are the disruptive Desktop Outsourcing technologies that enable your organization to radically change your business processes?
<--- Score

57. Identify an operational issue in your organization, for example, could a particular task be done more quickly or more efficiently by Desktop Outsourcing?
<--- Score

58. How often will data be collected for measures?
<--- Score

59. How do you promote understanding that opportunity for improvement is not criticism of the status quo, or the people who created the

status quo?
<--- Score

60. Have the problem and goal statements been updated to reflect the additional knowledge gained from the analyze phase?
<--- Score

61. Is there any way to speed up the process?
<--- Score

62. What will drive Desktop Outsourcing change?
<--- Score

63. What are the personnel training and qualifications required?
<--- Score

64. What conclusions were drawn from the team's data collection and analysis? How did the team reach these conclusions?
<--- Score

65. What are evaluation criteria for the output?
<--- Score

66. How do your work systems and key work processes relate to and capitalize on your core competencies?
<--- Score

67. Who qualifies to gain access to data?
<--- Score

68. Is the gap/opportunity displayed and communicated in financial terms?

<--- Score

69. Do several people in different organizational units assist with the Desktop Outsourcing process?
<--- Score

70. What are the necessary qualifications?
<--- Score

71. Are all team members qualified for all tasks?
<--- Score

72. Are you missing Desktop Outsourcing opportunities?
<--- Score

73. What other organizational variables, such as reward systems or communication systems, affect the performance of this Desktop Outsourcing process?
<--- Score

74. What are the processes for audit reporting and management?
<--- Score

75. Do you, as a leader, bounce back quickly from setbacks?
<--- Score

76. Can you add value to the current Desktop Outsourcing decision-making process (largely qualitative) by incorporating uncertainty modeling (more quantitative)?
<--- Score

77. Do your leaders quickly bounce back from

setbacks?
<--- Score

78. Record-keeping requirements flow from the records needed as inputs, outputs, controls and for transformation of a Desktop Outsourcing process, are the records needed as inputs to the Desktop Outsourcing process available?
<--- Score

79. What qualifies as competition?
<--- Score

80. What are your current levels and trends in key measures or indicators of Desktop Outsourcing product and process performance that are important to and directly serve your customers? How do these results compare with the performance of your competitors and other organizations with similar offerings?
<--- Score

81. Has an output goal been set?
<--- Score

82. What quality tools were used to get through the analyze phase?
<--- Score

83. What tools were used to generate the list of possible causes?
<--- Score

84. Were any designed experiments used to generate additional insight into the data analysis?
<--- Score

85. Should you invest in industry-recognized qualifications?
<--- Score

86. Are Desktop Outsourcing changes recognized early enough to be approved through the regular process?
<--- Score

87. What do you need to qualify?
<--- Score

88. Is the performance gap determined?
<--- Score

89. How do you ensure that the Desktop Outsourcing opportunity is realistic?
<--- Score

90. Which Desktop Outsourcing data should be retained?
<--- Score

91. How was the detailed process map generated, verified, and validated?
<--- Score

92. How do mission and objectives affect the Desktop Outsourcing processes of your organization?
<--- Score

93. Do your contracts/agreements contain data security obligations?
<--- Score

94. Were there any improvement opportunities identified from the process analysis?
<--- Score

95. What output to create?
<--- Score

96. Do you have the authority to produce the output?
<--- Score

97. How will the Desktop Outsourcing data be captured?
<--- Score

98. What data is gathered?
<--- Score

99. Have you defined which data is gathered how?
<--- Score

100. Who will facilitate the team and process?
<--- Score

101. Where is the data coming from to measure compliance?
<--- Score

102. What are your best practices for minimizing Desktop Outsourcing project risk, while demonstrating incremental value and quick wins throughout the Desktop Outsourcing project lifecycle?
<--- Score

103. What qualifications are necessary?
<--- Score

104. Was a cause-and-effect diagram used to explore the different types of causes (or sources of variation)?
<--- Score

105. How will corresponding data be collected?
<--- Score

106. What Desktop Outsourcing data should be collected?
<--- Score

107. What are your outputs?
<--- Score

108. What types of data do your Desktop Outsourcing indicators require?
<--- Score

109. What qualifications are needed?
<--- Score

110. Where can you get qualified talent today?
<--- Score

111. How much data can be collected in the given timeframe?
<--- Score

112. What methods do you use to gather Desktop Outsourcing data?
<--- Score

113. What is your organizations system for selecting qualified vendors?
<--- Score

114. What other jobs or tasks affect the performance of the steps in the Desktop Outsourcing process?
<--- Score

115. Who owns what data?
<--- Score

116. How do you identify specific Desktop Outsourcing investment opportunities and emerging trends?
<--- Score

117. What are your key performance measures or indicators and in-process measures for the control and improvement of your Desktop Outsourcing processes?
<--- Score

118. How difficult is it to qualify what Desktop Outsourcing ROI is?
<--- Score

119. Is data and process analysis, root cause analysis and quantifying the gap/opportunity in place?
<--- Score

120. Is the required Desktop Outsourcing data gathered?
<--- Score

121. How are outputs preserved and protected?
<--- Score

122. Is the final output clearly identified?
<--- Score

123. What is the Desktop Outsourcing Driver?
<--- Score

124. What process should you select for improvement?
<--- Score

125. What Desktop Outsourcing data do you gather or use now?
<--- Score

126. What is the cost of poor quality as supported by the team's analysis?
<--- Score

127. What is your organizations process which leads to recognition of value generation?
<--- Score

128. Do your employees have the opportunity to do what they do best everyday?
<--- Score

129. What is the complexity of the output produced?
<--- Score

130. What process improvements will be needed?
<--- Score

Add up total points for this section:
_ _ _ _ _ = Total points for this section

Divided by: _ _ _ _ _ _ (number of statements answered) = _ _ _ _ _ _
Average score for this section

Transfer your score to the Desktop
Outsourcing Index at the beginning of
the Self-Assessment.

CRITERION #5: IMPROVE:

INTENT: Develop a practical solution.
Innovate, establish and test the
solution and to measure the results.

In my belief, the answer to this
question is clearly defined:

5 Strongly Agree

4 Agree

3 Neutral

2 Disagree

1 Strongly Disagree

1. What are the implications of the one critical
Desktop Outsourcing decision 10 minutes, 10 months,
and 10 years from now?
<--- Score

2. Have you identified breakpoints and/or risk
tolerances that will trigger broad consideration of
a potential need for intervention or modification
of strategy?

<--- Score

3. Do you combine technical expertise with business knowledge and Desktop Outsourcing Key topics include lifecycles, development approaches, requirements and how to make a business case?
<--- Score

4. What tools were used to tap into the creativity and encourage 'outside the box' thinking?
<--- Score

5. What were the underlying assumptions on the cost-benefit analysis?
<--- Score

6. Where do you need Desktop Outsourcing improvement?
<--- Score

7. How do you go about comparing Desktop Outsourcing approaches/solutions?
<--- Score

8. Can you integrate quality management and risk management?
<--- Score

9. Were any criteria developed to assist the team in testing and evaluating potential solutions?
<--- Score

10. What is the implementation plan?
<--- Score

11. Is there any other Desktop Outsourcing solution?

<--- Score

12. How do you decide how much to remunerate an employee?
<--- Score

13. Who will be responsible for documenting the Desktop Outsourcing requirements in detail?
<--- Score

14. What are the Desktop Outsourcing security risks?
<--- Score

15. How will you recognize and celebrate results?
<--- Score

16. What strategies for Desktop Outsourcing improvement are successful?
<--- Score

17. How can you improve performance?
<--- Score

18. Is supporting Desktop Outsourcing documentation required?
<--- Score

19. What practices helps your organization to develop its capacity to recognize patterns?
<--- Score

20. What is the team's contingency plan for potential problems occurring in implementation?
<--- Score

21. Are the key business and technology risks being

managed?
<--- Score

22. What are the concrete Desktop Outsourcing results?
<--- Score

23. How do you keep improving Desktop Outsourcing?
<--- Score

24. What is the magnitude of the improvements?
<--- Score

25. Does the goal represent a desired result that can be measured?
<--- Score

26. Are events managed to resolution?
<--- Score

27. To what extent does management recognize Desktop Outsourcing as a tool to increase the results?
<--- Score

28. Who manages Desktop Outsourcing risk?
<--- Score

29. Is any Desktop Outsourcing documentation required?
<--- Score

30. What improvements have been achieved?
<--- Score

31. Risk events: what are the things that could go

wrong?
<--- Score

32. Who are the Desktop Outsourcing decision-makers?
<--- Score

33. How can you improve Desktop Outsourcing?
<--- Score

34. How are policy decisions made and where?
<--- Score

35. How risky is your organization?
<--- Score

36. Which of the recognised risks out of all risks can be most likely transferred?
<--- Score

37. What communications are necessary to support the implementation of the solution?
<--- Score

38. Have you achieved Desktop Outsourcing improvements?
<--- Score

39. Who do you report Desktop Outsourcing results to?
<--- Score

40. What risks do you need to manage?
<--- Score

41. Who are the key stakeholders for the Desktop

Outsourcing evaluation?
<--- Score

42. Is risk periodically assessed?
<--- Score

43. What area needs the greatest improvement?
<--- Score

44. What is the Desktop Outsourcing's sustainability risk?
<--- Score

45. What tools do you use once you have decided on a Desktop Outsourcing strategy and more importantly how do you choose?
<--- Score

46. Is the implementation plan designed?
<--- Score

47. Are you assessing Desktop Outsourcing and risk?
<--- Score

48. Are decisions made in a timely manner?
<--- Score

49. Is the optimal solution selected based on testing and analysis?
<--- Score

50. Is a solution implementation plan established, including schedule/work breakdown structure, resources, risk management plan, cost/budget, and control plan?
<--- Score

51. Who will be using the results of the measurement activities?

<--- Score

52. What are the expected Desktop Outsourcing results?

<--- Score

53. Desktop Outsourcing risk decisions: whose call Is It?

<--- Score

54. How do you define the solutions' scope?

<--- Score

55. How do you mitigate Desktop Outsourcing risk?

<--- Score

56. How do you improve Desktop Outsourcing service perception, and satisfaction?

<--- Score

57. Who are the Desktop Outsourcing decision makers?

<--- Score

58. What tools were used to evaluate the potential solutions?

<--- Score

59. How will you know that a change is an improvement?

<--- Score

60. How significant is the improvement in the eyes of

the end user?

<--- Score

61. What criteria will you use to assess your Desktop Outsourcing risks?

<--- Score

62. Who should make the Desktop Outsourcing decisions?

<--- Score

63. What is Desktop Outsourcing's impact on utilizing the best solution(s)?

<--- Score

64. Is there a cost/benefit analysis of optimal solution(s)?

<--- Score

65. Is there a high likelihood that any recommendations will achieve their intended results?

<--- Score

66. Are risk management tasks balanced centrally and locally?

<--- Score

67. Which Desktop Outsourcing solution is appropriate?

<--- Score

68. How is continuous improvement applied to risk management?

<--- Score

69. Who will be responsible for making the decisions to include or exclude requested changes once Desktop Outsourcing is underway?
<--- Score

70. What needs improvement? Why?
<--- Score

71. Is a contingency plan established?
<--- Score

72. Explorations of the frontiers of Desktop Outsourcing will help you build influence, improve Desktop Outsourcing, optimize decision making, and sustain change, what is your approach?
<--- Score

73. Is pilot data collected and analyzed?
<--- Score

74. Where do the Desktop Outsourcing decisions reside?
<--- Score

75. Is there a small-scale pilot for proposed improvement(s)? What conclusions were drawn from the outcomes of a pilot?
<--- Score

76. Who manages supplier risk management in your organization?
<--- Score

77. Is the scope clearly documented?
<--- Score

78. Do you need to do a usability evaluation?
<--- Score

79. What does the 'should be' process map/design look like?
<--- Score

80. Do you cover the five essential competencies: Communication, Collaboration,Innovation, Adaptability, and Leadership that improve an organizations ability to leverage the new Desktop Outsourcing in a volatile global economy?
<--- Score

81. Who are the people involved in developing and implementing Desktop Outsourcing?
<--- Score

82. Is Desktop Outsourcing documentation maintained?
<--- Score

83. How do you measure improved Desktop Outsourcing service perception, and satisfaction?
<--- Score

84. How do the Desktop Outsourcing results compare with the performance of your competitors and other organizations with similar offerings?
<--- Score

85. Risk factors: what are the characteristics of Desktop Outsourcing that make it risky?
<--- Score

86. Is the measure of success for Desktop Outsourcing understandable to a variety of people?
<--- Score

87. How does your organization evaluate strategic Desktop Outsourcing success?
<--- Score

88. How are Desktop Outsourcing risks managed?
<--- Score

89. How do you measure progress and evaluate training effectiveness?
<--- Score

90. Would you develop a Desktop Outsourcing Communication Strategy?
<--- Score

91. Is the Desktop Outsourcing solution sustainable?
<--- Score

92. How do you improve productivity?
<--- Score

93. How can the phases of Desktop Outsourcing development be identified?
<--- Score

94. What assumptions are made about the solution and approach?
<--- Score

95. Who do you report Desktop Outsourcing results to?
<--- Score

96. What do you want to improve?
<--- Score

97. How can you better manage risk?
<--- Score

98. Does a good decision guarantee a good outcome?
<--- Score

99. What alternative responses are available to manage risk?
<--- Score

100. For decision problems, how do you develop a decision statement?
<--- Score

101. Can the solution be designed and implemented within an acceptable time period?
<--- Score

102. What resources are required for the improvement efforts?
<--- Score

103. How will you measure the results?
<--- Score

104. Is the Desktop Outsourcing risk managed?
<--- Score

105. How do you improve your likelihood of success ?
<--- Score

106. What is Desktop Outsourcing risk?

<--- Score

107. What to do with the results or outcomes of measurements?

<--- Score

108. How will you know when its improved?

<--- Score

109. What error proofing will be done to address some of the discrepancies observed in the 'as is' process?

<--- Score

110. What can you do to improve?

<--- Score

111. What Desktop Outsourcing improvements can be made?

<--- Score

112. What were the criteria for evaluating a Desktop Outsourcing pilot?

<--- Score

113. What actually has to improve and by how much?

<--- Score

114. Can you identify any significant risks or exposures to Desktop Outsourcing third- parties (vendors, service providers, alliance partners etc) that concern you?

<--- Score

115. What should a proof of concept or pilot accomplish?

<--- Score

116. In the past few months, what is the smallest change you have made that has had the biggest positive result? What was it about that small change that produced the large return?

<--- Score

117. Who controls key decisions that will be made?

<--- Score

118. Who makes the Desktop Outsourcing decisions in your organization?

<--- Score

119. How do you link measurement and risk?

<--- Score

120. What is the risk?

<--- Score

121. What went well, what should change, what can improve?

<--- Score

122. Are the most efficient solutions problem-specific?

<--- Score

123. Do vendor agreements bring new compliance risk ?

<--- Score

124. How is knowledge sharing about risk management improved?

<--- Score

125. What attendant changes will need to be made to ensure that the solution is successful?
<--- Score

126. How do you manage and improve your Desktop Outsourcing work systems to deliver customer value and achieve organizational success and sustainability?
<--- Score

127. How scalable is your Desktop Outsourcing solution?
<--- Score

128. At what point will vulnerability assessments be performed once Desktop Outsourcing is put into production (e.g., ongoing Risk Management after implementation)?
<--- Score

129. Are risk triggers captured?
<--- Score

130. What tools were most useful during the improve phase?
<--- Score

131. How does the team improve its work?
<--- Score

132. How do you manage Desktop Outsourcing risk?
<--- Score

133. Do those selected for the Desktop Outsourcing team have a good general understanding of what

Desktop Outsourcing is all about?
<--- Score

134. What lessons, if any, from a pilot were incorporated into the design of the full-scale solution?
<--- Score

135. Was a pilot designed for the proposed solution(s)?
<--- Score

136. How do you measure risk?
<--- Score

137. Will the controls trigger any other risks?
<--- Score

138. What are your current levels and trends in key measures or indicators of workforce and leader development?
<--- Score

139. How do you deal with Desktop Outsourcing risk?
<--- Score

140. How risky is your organization?
<--- Score

141. For estimation problems, how do you develop an estimation statement?
<--- Score

142. What are the affordable Desktop Outsourcing risks?
<--- Score

Add up total points for this section:
_____ = Total points for this section

Divided by: _____ (number of
statements answered) = _____
Average score for this section

Transfer your score to the Desktop
Outsourcing Index at the beginning of
the Self-Assessment.

CRITERION #6: CONTROL:

INTENT: Implement the practical solution. Maintain the performance and correct possible complications.

In my belief, the answer to this question is clearly defined:

5 Strongly Agree

4 Agree

3 Neutral

2 Disagree

1 Strongly Disagree

1. Act/Adjust: What Do you Need to Do Differently?
<--- Score

2. Is a response plan in place for when the input, process, or output measures indicate an 'out-of-control' condition?
<--- Score

3. What are your results for key measures or indicators

of the accomplishment of your Desktop Outsourcing strategy and action plans, including building and strengthening core competencies?
<--- Score

4. Will any special training be provided for results interpretation?
<--- Score

5. Are the Desktop Outsourcing standards challenging?
<--- Score

6. What quality tools were useful in the control phase?
<--- Score

7. What is the recommended frequency of auditing?
<--- Score

8. Is there a documented and implemented monitoring plan?
<--- Score

9. How do your controls stack up?
<--- Score

10. Is knowledge gained on process shared and institutionalized?
<--- Score

11. Is a response plan established and deployed?
<--- Score

12. Has the Desktop Outsourcing value of standards been quantified?
<--- Score

13. Against what alternative is success being measured?
<--- Score

14. Will the team be available to assist members in planning investigations?
<--- Score

15. What are the known security controls?
<--- Score

16. How will the day-to-day responsibilities for monitoring and continual improvement be transferred from the improvement team to the process owner?
<--- Score

17. Can support from partners be adjusted?
<--- Score

18. Are the planned controls working?
<--- Score

19. Are there documented procedures?
<--- Score

20. Is there documentation that will support the successful operation of the improvement?
<--- Score

21. Does the response plan contain a definite closed loop continual improvement scheme (e.g., plan-do-check-act)?
<--- Score

22. How do you plan on providing proper recognition and disclosure of supporting companies?
<--- Score

23. How will you measure your QA plan's effectiveness?
<--- Score

24. How will the process owner and team be able to hold the gains?
<--- Score

25. In the case of a Desktop Outsourcing project, the criteria for the audit derive from implementation objectives, an audit of a Desktop Outsourcing project involves assessing whether the recommendations outlined for implementation have been met, can you track that any Desktop Outsourcing project is implemented as planned, and is it working?
<--- Score

26. Is there a standardized process?
<--- Score

27. Are controls in place and consistently applied?
<--- Score

28. How do you spread information?
<--- Score

29. How will new or emerging customer needs/requirements be checked/communicated to orient the process toward meeting the new specifications and continually reducing variation?
<--- Score

30. How do you encourage people to take control and responsibility?
<--- Score

31. Are the planned controls in place?
<--- Score

32. What should the next improvement project be that is related to Desktop Outsourcing?
<--- Score

33. Will your goals reflect your program budget?
<--- Score

34. Do you monitor the effectiveness of your Desktop Outsourcing activities?
<--- Score

35. How might the group capture best practices and lessons learned so as to leverage improvements?
<--- Score

36. Will existing staff require re-training, for example, to learn new business processes?
<--- Score

37. What other areas of the group might benefit from the Desktop Outsourcing team's improvements, knowledge, and learning?
<--- Score

38. How is change control managed?
<--- Score

39. Are new process steps, standards, and documentation ingrained into normal operations?

<--- Score

40. How is Desktop Outsourcing project cost planned, managed, monitored?
<--- Score

41. How will the process owner verify improvement in present and future sigma levels, process capabilities?
<--- Score

42. What are the key elements of your Desktop Outsourcing performance improvement system, including your evaluation, organizational learning, and innovation processes?
<--- Score

43. Can you adapt and adjust to changing Desktop Outsourcing situations?
<--- Score

44. How widespread is its use?
<--- Score

45. Is reporting being used or needed?
<--- Score

46. What is your plan to assess your security risks?
<--- Score

47. What is the standard for acceptable Desktop Outsourcing performance?
<--- Score

48. How can you best use all of your knowledge repositories to enhance learning and sharing?
<--- Score

49. What are the performance and scale of the Desktop Outsourcing tools?
<--- Score

50. How will report readings be checked to effectively monitor performance?
<--- Score

51. What key inputs and outputs are being measured on an ongoing basis?
<--- Score

52. Is there a recommended audit plan for routine surveillance inspections of Desktop Outsourcing's gains?
<--- Score

53. How do controls support value?
<--- Score

54. Are suggested corrective/restorative actions indicated on the response plan for known causes to problems that might surface?
<--- Score

55. Who is going to spread your message?
<--- Score

56. Who is the Desktop Outsourcing process owner?
<--- Score

57. Do the Desktop Outsourcing decisions you make today help people and the planet tomorrow?
<--- Score

58. Where do ideas that reach policy makers and planners as proposals for Desktop Outsourcing strengthening and reform actually originate?
<--- Score

59. What are the critical parameters to watch?
<--- Score

60. Who controls critical resources?
<--- Score

61. How do you select, collect, align, and integrate Desktop Outsourcing data and information for tracking daily operations and overall organizational performance, including progress relative to strategic objectives and action plans?
<--- Score

62. How do senior leaders actions reflect a commitment to the organizations Desktop Outsourcing values?
<--- Score

63. How do you plan for the cost of succession?
<--- Score

64. Is there a Desktop Outsourcing Communication plan covering who needs to get what information when?
<--- Score

65. What are customers monitoring?
<--- Score

66. Does the Desktop Outsourcing performance meet the customer's requirements?

<--- Score

67. Have new or revised work instructions resulted?
<--- Score

68. Are you measuring, monitoring and predicting Desktop Outsourcing activities to optimize operations and profitability, and enhancing outcomes?
<--- Score

69. Does job training on the documented procedures need to be part of the process team's education and training?
<--- Score

70. Who will be in control?
<--- Score

71. Do the viable solutions scale to future needs?
<--- Score

72. Has the improved process and its steps been standardized?
<--- Score

73. What adjustments to the strategies are needed?
<--- Score

74. You may have created your quality measures at a time when you lacked resources, technology wasn't up to the required standard, or low service levels were the industry norm. Have those circumstances changed?
<--- Score

75. Does a troubleshooting guide exist or is it needed?

<--- Score

76. How likely is the current Desktop Outsourcing plan to come in on schedule or on budget?
<--- Score

77. How do you establish and deploy modified action plans if circumstances require a shift in plans and rapid execution of new plans?
<--- Score

78. Are operating procedures consistent?
<--- Score

79. What can you control?
<--- Score

80. Is new knowledge gained imbedded in the response plan?
<--- Score

81. Implementation Planning: is a pilot needed to test the changes before a full roll out occurs?
<--- Score

82. Is there a control plan in place for sustaining improvements (short and long-term)?
<--- Score

83. How do you monitor usage and cost?
<--- Score

84. Who has control over resources?
<--- Score

85. What do you stand for--and what are you against?

<--- Score

86. How will Desktop Outsourcing decisions be made and monitored?
<--- Score

87. What other systems, operations, processes, and infrastructures (hiring practices, staffing, training, incentives/rewards, metrics/dashboards/scorecards, etc.) need updates, additions, changes, or deletions in order to facilitate knowledge transfer and improvements?
<--- Score

88. Are pertinent alerts monitored, analyzed and distributed to appropriate personnel?
<--- Score

89. What do you measure to verify effectiveness gains?
<--- Score

90. What should you measure to verify efficiency gains?
<--- Score

91. What is the best design framework for Desktop Outsourcing organization now that, in a post industrial-age if the top-down, command and control model is no longer relevant?
<--- Score

92. Are documented procedures clear and easy to follow for the operators?
<--- Score

93. What is your theory of human motivation, and how does your compensation plan fit with that view?
<--- Score

94. What are you attempting to measure/monitor?
<--- Score

95. What do your reports reflect?
<--- Score

96. Is there an action plan in case of emergencies?
<--- Score

97. Is there a transfer of ownership and knowledge to process owner and process team tasked with the responsibilities.
<--- Score

98. Do you monitor the Desktop Outsourcing decisions made and fine tune them as they evolve?
<--- Score

99. How will input, process, and output variables be checked to detect for sub-optimal conditions?
<--- Score

100. What is the control/monitoring plan?
<--- Score

Add up total points for this section:
_____ = Total points for this section

Divided by: _____ (number of statements answered) = _____
Average score for this section

Transfer your score to the Desktop Outsourcing Index at the beginning of the Self-Assessment.

CRITERION #7: SUSTAIN:

INTENT: Retain the benefits.

In my belief, the answer to this question is clearly defined:

5 Strongly Agree

4 Agree

3 Neutral

2 Disagree

1 Strongly Disagree

1. If you do not follow, then how to lead?
<--- Score

2. Who do we want your customers to become?
<--- Score

3. What is your BATNA (best alternative to a negotiated agreement)?
<--- Score

4. Ask yourself: how would you do this work if you

only had one staff member to do it?
<--- Score

5. Are all key stakeholders present at all Structured Walkthroughs?
<--- Score

6. What are the potential basics of Desktop Outsourcing fraud?
<--- Score

7. Is Desktop Outsourcing realistic, or are you setting yourself up for failure?
<--- Score

8. Operational - will it work?
<--- Score

9. What are the barriers to increased Desktop Outsourcing production?
<--- Score

10. Marketing budgets are tighter, consumers are more skeptical, and social media has changed forever the way we talk about Desktop Outsourcing, how do you gain traction?
<--- Score

11. Do you have past Desktop Outsourcing successes?
<--- Score

12. How are you doing compared to your industry?
<--- Score

13. Can you break it down?
<--- Score

14. Who will be responsible for deciding whether Desktop Outsourcing goes ahead or not after the initial investigations?
<--- Score

15. How do you set Desktop Outsourcing stretch targets and how do you get people to not only participate in setting these stretch targets but also that they strive to achieve these?
<--- Score

16. What are the top 3 things at the forefront of your Desktop Outsourcing agendas for the next 3 years?
<--- Score

17. How do you know if you are successful?
<--- Score

18. What is your competitive advantage?
<--- Score

19. What are strategies for increasing support and reducing opposition?
<--- Score

20. How do you create buy-in?
<--- Score

21. What must you excel at?
<--- Score

22. Can you maintain your growth without detracting from the factors that have contributed to your success?
<--- Score

23. What is your question? Why?
<--- Score

24. How do you make it meaningful in connecting Desktop Outsourcing with what users do day-to-day?
<--- Score

25. What goals did you miss?
<--- Score

26. How do you proactively clarify deliverables and Desktop Outsourcing quality expectations?
<--- Score

27. Are you maintaining a past–present–future perspective throughout the Desktop Outsourcing discussion?
<--- Score

28. What does your signature ensure?
<--- Score

29. Who have you, as a company, historically been when you've been at your best?
<--- Score

30. How do you accomplish your long range Desktop Outsourcing goals?
<--- Score

31. Why do and why don't your customers like your organization?
<--- Score

32. How do you govern and fulfill your societal

responsibilities?
<--- Score

33. What is the overall talent health of your organization as a whole at senior levels, and for each organization reporting to a member of the Senior Leadership Team?
<--- Score

34. What are the gaps in your knowledge and experience?
<--- Score

35. How likely is it that a customer would recommend your company to a friend or colleague?
<--- Score

36. If no one would ever find out about your accomplishments, how would you lead differently?
<--- Score

37. What did you miss in the interview for the worst hire you ever made?
<--- Score

38. How do you maintain Desktop Outsourcing's Integrity?
<--- Score

39. Why is it important to have senior management support for a Desktop Outsourcing project?
<--- Score

40. What are your personal philosophies regarding Desktop Outsourcing and how do they influence your work?

<--- Score

41. How do you foster the skills, knowledge, talents, attributes, and characteristics you want to have?
<--- Score

42. What is the funding source for this project?
<--- Score

43. Do you have the right capabilities and capacities?
<--- Score

44. Who is on the team?
<--- Score

45. How do you ensure that implementations of Desktop Outsourcing products are done in a way that ensures safety?
<--- Score

46. How do you transition from the baseline to the target?
<--- Score

47. How do you deal with Desktop Outsourcing changes?
<--- Score

48. Can you do all this work?
<--- Score

49. What are your most important goals for the strategic Desktop Outsourcing objectives?
<--- Score

50. What are specific Desktop Outsourcing rules to follow?
<--- Score

51. Who is the main stakeholder, with ultimate responsibility for driving Desktop Outsourcing forward?
<--- Score

52. What could happen if you do not do it?
<--- Score

53. Are you making progress, and are you making progress as Desktop Outsourcing leaders?
<--- Score

54. How do you engage the workforce, in addition to satisfying them?
<--- Score

55. Is there any reason to believe the opposite of my current belief?
<--- Score

56. How do you provide a safe environment -physically and emotionally?
<--- Score

57. Who are the key stakeholders?
<--- Score

58. What are the key enablers to make this Desktop Outsourcing move?
<--- Score

59. Who will provide the final approval of Desktop

Outsourcing deliverables?

<--- Score

60. If there were zero limitations, what would you do differently?

<--- Score

61. To whom do you add value?

<--- Score

62. Political -is anyone trying to undermine this project?

<--- Score

63. What are the short and long-term Desktop Outsourcing goals?

<--- Score

64. Is maximizing Desktop Outsourcing protection the same as minimizing Desktop Outsourcing loss?

<--- Score

65. What are the success criteria that will indicate that Desktop Outsourcing objectives have been met and the benefits delivered?

<--- Score

66. What is your Desktop Outsourcing strategy?

<--- Score

67. Are assumptions made in Desktop Outsourcing stated explicitly?

<--- Score

68. What is the overall business strategy?

<--- Score

69. What are the essentials of internal Desktop Outsourcing management?
<--- Score

70. Are the assumptions believable and achievable?
<--- Score

71. What role does communication play in the success or failure of a Desktop Outsourcing project?
<--- Score

72. What is a feasible sequencing of reform initiatives over time?
<--- Score

73. How do you keep the momentum going?
<--- Score

74. How do you stay inspired?
<--- Score

75. How do you lead with Desktop Outsourcing in mind?
<--- Score

76. How is implementation research currently incorporated into each of your goals?
<--- Score

77. What are the usability implications of Desktop Outsourcing actions?
<--- Score

78. What is the recommended frequency of auditing?

<--- Score

79. What trophy do you want on your mantle?
<--- Score

80. What business benefits will Desktop Outsourcing goals deliver if achieved?
<--- Score

81. Why is Desktop Outsourcing important for you now?
<--- Score

82. What one word do you want to own in the minds of your customers, employees, and partners?
<--- Score

83. Would you rather sell to knowledgeable and informed customers or to uninformed customers?
<--- Score

84. What is the kind of project structure that would be appropriate for your Desktop Outsourcing project, should it be formal and complex, or can it be less formal and relatively simple?
<--- Score

85. Why will customers want to buy your organizations products/services?
<--- Score

86. What are internal and external Desktop Outsourcing relations?
<--- Score

87. What are current Desktop Outsourcing

paradigms?

<--- Score

88. What should you stop doing?

<--- Score

89. Are you satisfied with your current role? If not, what is missing from it?

<--- Score

90. How do you determine the key elements that affect Desktop Outsourcing workforce satisfaction, how are these elements determined for different workforce groups and segments?

<--- Score

91. At what moment would you think; Will I get fired?

<--- Score

92. Think of your Desktop Outsourcing project, what are the main functions?

<--- Score

93. Do you feel that more should be done in the Desktop Outsourcing area?

<--- Score

94. What is the range of capabilities?

<--- Score

95. What happens at your organization when people fail?

<--- Score

96. How will you ensure you get what you expected?

<--- Score

97. What happens if you do not have enough funding?
<--- Score

98. If you had to leave your organization for a year and the only communication you could have with employees/colleagues was a single paragraph, what would you write?
<--- Score

99. Why not do Desktop Outsourcing?
<--- Score

100. What are the rules and assumptions your industry operates under? What if the opposite were true?
<--- Score

101. How can you negotiate Desktop Outsourcing successfully with a stubborn boss, an irate client, or a deceitful coworker?
<--- Score

102. How do you manage Desktop Outsourcing Knowledge Management (KM)?
<--- Score

103. What would you recommend your friend do if he/she were facing this dilemma?
<--- Score

104. If you were responsible for initiating and implementing major changes in your organization, what steps might you take to ensure acceptance of those changes?

<--- Score

105. Who do you think the world wants your organization to be?
<--- Score

106. What current systems have to be understood and/or changed?
<--- Score

107. Whose voice (department, ethnic group, women, older workers, etc) might you have missed hearing from in your company, and how might you amplify this voice to create positive momentum for your business?
<--- Score

108. What are the challenges?
<--- Score

109. If you got fired and a new hire took your place, what would she do different?
<--- Score

110. What may be the consequences for the performance of an organization if all stakeholders are not consulted regarding Desktop Outsourcing?
<--- Score

111. If you find that you havent accomplished one of the goals for one of the steps of the Desktop Outsourcing strategy, what will you do to fix it?
<--- Score

112. What have been your experiences in defining long range Desktop Outsourcing goals?

<--- Score

113. How do you keep records, of what?
<--- Score

114. Is a Desktop Outsourcing team work effort in place?
<--- Score

115. What happens when a new employee joins the organization?
<--- Score

116. What information is critical to your organization that your executives are ignoring?
<--- Score

117. How will you motivate the stakeholders with the least vested interest?
<--- Score

118. Do you think you know, or do you know you know ?
<--- Score

119. What knowledge, skills and characteristics mark a good Desktop Outsourcing project manager?
<--- Score

120. If you weren't already in this business, would you enter it today? And if not, what are you going to do about it?
<--- Score

121. What are the business goals Desktop Outsourcing is aiming to achieve?

<--- Score

122. Is your basic point _____ or _____?
<--- Score

123. Is there a work around that you can use?
<--- Score

124. How can you incorporate support to ensure safe and effective use of Desktop Outsourcing into the services that you provide?
<--- Score

125. What stupid rule would you most like to kill?
<--- Score

126. Is Desktop Outsourcing dependent on the successful delivery of a current project?
<--- Score

127. What will be the consequences to the stakeholder (financial, reputation etc) if Desktop Outsourcing does not go ahead or fails to deliver the objectives?
<--- Score

128. Is the Desktop Outsourcing organization completing tasks effectively and efficiently?
<--- Score

129. What are you challenging?
<--- Score

130. Are the criteria for selecting recommendations stated?
<--- Score

131. How long will it take to change?
<--- Score

132. Who are your customers?
<--- Score

133. Who, on the executive team or the board, has spoken to a customer recently?
<--- Score

134. Will it be accepted by users?
<--- Score

135. How do you foster innovation?
<--- Score

136. How do you track customer value, profitability or financial return, organizational success, and sustainability?
<--- Score

137. How do you go about securing Desktop Outsourcing?
<--- Score

138. Instead of going to current contacts for new ideas, what if you reconnected with dormant contacts--the people you used to know? If you were going reactivate a dormant tie, who would it be?
<--- Score

139. What management system can you use to leverage the Desktop Outsourcing experience, ideas, and concerns of the people closest to the work to be done?

<--- Score

140. Which functions and people interact with the supplier and or customer?
<--- Score

141. What would have to be true for the option on the table to be the best possible choice?
<--- Score

142. Why should people listen to you?
<--- Score

143. Who will determine interim and final deadlines?
<--- Score

144. What potential megatrends could make your business model obsolete?
<--- Score

145. Do you think Desktop Outsourcing accomplishes the goals you expect it to accomplish?
<--- Score

146. What new services of functionality will be implemented next with Desktop Outsourcing ?
<--- Score

147. How can you become the company that would put you out of business?
<--- Score

148. If your company went out of business tomorrow, would anyone who doesn't get a paycheck here care?
<--- Score

149. In the past year, what have you done (or could you have done) to increase the accurate perception of your company/brand as ethical and honest?
<--- Score

150. What projects are going on in the organization today, and what resources are those projects using from the resource pools?
<--- Score

151. Which models, tools and techniques are necessary?
<--- Score

152. Are you / should you be revolutionary or evolutionary?
<--- Score

153. Who uses your product in ways you never expected?
<--- Score

154. What you are going to do to affect the numbers?
<--- Score

155. How will you insure seamless interoperability of Desktop Outsourcing moving forward?
<--- Score

156. What trouble can you get into?
<--- Score

157. When information truly is ubiquitous, when reach and connectivity are completely global, when computing resources are infinite, and when a whole new set of impossibilities are not only possible, but

happening, what will that do to your business?
<--- Score

158. How do senior leaders deploy your organizations vision and values through your leadership system, to the workforce, to key suppliers and partners, and to customers and other stakeholders, as appropriate?
<--- Score

159. Will there be any necessary staff changes (redundancies or new hires)?
<--- Score

160. What is the estimated value of the project?
<--- Score

161. If you had to rebuild your organization without any traditional competitive advantages (i.e., no killer technology, promising research, innovative product/service delivery model, etcetera), how would your people have to approach their work and collaborate together in order to create the necessary conditions for success?
<--- Score

162. Who are four people whose careers you have enhanced?
<--- Score

163. How much contingency will be available in the budget?
<--- Score

164. What is an unauthorized commitment?

<--- Score

165. Where can you break convention?
<--- Score

166. Who else should you help?
<--- Score

167. How important is Desktop Outsourcing to the user organizations mission?
<--- Score

168. Do you have enough freaky customers in your portfolio pushing you to the limit day in and day out?
<--- Score

169. What is the craziest thing you can do?
<--- Score

170. In a project to restructure Desktop Outsourcing outcomes, which stakeholders would you involve?
<--- Score

171. How will you know that the Desktop Outsourcing project has been successful?
<--- Score

172. What is it like to work for you?
<--- Score

173. What unique value proposition (UVP) do you offer?
<--- Score

174. What is the purpose of Desktop Outsourcing in relation to the mission?

<--- Score

175. In retrospect, of the projects that you pulled the plug on, what percent do you wish had been allowed to keep going, and what percent do you wish had ended earlier?

<--- Score

176. What was the last experiment you ran?

<--- Score

177. Who is responsible for errors?

<--- Score

178. What is the source of the strategies for Desktop Outsourcing strengthening and reform?

<--- Score

179. What relationships among Desktop Outsourcing trends do you perceive?

<--- Score

180. What is your formula for success in Desktop Outsourcing ?

<--- Score

181. Is your strategy driving your strategy? Or is the way in which you allocate resources driving your strategy?

<--- Score

182. What are you trying to prove to yourself, and how might it be hijacking your life and business success?

<--- Score

183. Is there any existing Desktop Outsourcing governance structure?
<--- Score

184. Can the schedule be done in the given time?
<--- Score

185. What Desktop Outsourcing modifications can you make work for you?
<--- Score

Add up total points for this section:
_____ = Total points for this section

Divided by: _____ (number of statements answered) = _____
Average score for this section

Transfer your score to the Desktop Outsourcing Index at the beginning of the Self-Assessment.

Desktop Outsourcing and Managing Projects, Criteria for Project Managers:

1.0 Initiating Process Group: Desktop Outsourcing

1. How well did the chosen processes fit the needs of the Desktop Outsourcing project?

2. Will the Desktop Outsourcing project meet the client requirements, and will it achieve the business success criteria that justified doing the Desktop Outsourcing project in the first place?

3. During which stage of Risk planning are risks prioritized based on probability and impact?

4. Have you evaluated the teams performance and asked for feedback?

5. Are stakeholders properly informed about the status of the Desktop Outsourcing project?

6. Do you know the roles & responsibilities required for this Desktop Outsourcing project?

7. What were things that you did well, and could improve, and how?

8. Who is behind the Desktop Outsourcing project?

9. Realistic - are the desired results expressed in a way that the team will be motivated and believe that the required level of involvement will be obtained?

10. What will be the pressing issues of tomorrow?

11. Are identified risks being monitored properly, are

new risks arising during the Desktop Outsourcing project or are foreseen risks occurring?

12. Does it make any difference if you am successful?

13. At which stage, in a typical Desktop Outsourcing project do stake holders have maximum influence?

14. Were decisions made in a timely manner?

15. What are the overarching issues of your organization?

16. Do you know if the Desktop Outsourcing project requires outside equipment or vendor resources?

17. What will you do?

18. Specific - is the objective clear in terms of what, how, when, and where the situation will be changed?

19. When are the deliverables to be generated in each phase?

20. Are there resources to maintain and support the outcome of the Desktop Outsourcing project?

1.1 Project Charter: Desktop Outsourcing

21. Strategic fit: what is the strategic initiative identifier for this Desktop Outsourcing project?

22. What is in it for you?

23. What is the most common tool for helping define the detail?

24. What are the assumptions?

25. Who is the sponsor?

26. When will this occur?

27. Why is a Desktop Outsourcing project Charter used?

28. Desktop Outsourcing project deliverables: what is the Desktop Outsourcing project going to produce?

29. Where and how does the team fit within your organization structure?

30. What is the purpose of the Desktop Outsourcing project?

31. How high should you set your goals?

32. What are you trying to accomplish?

33. How will you learn more about the process or system you are trying to improve?

34. Why use a Desktop Outsourcing project charter?

35. Avoid costs, improve service, and/ or comply with a mandate?

36. Will this replace an existing product?

37. Why do you need to manage scope?

38. What is the justification?

39. If finished, on what date did it finish?

40. Market – identify products market, including whether it is outside of the objective: what is the purpose of the program or Desktop Outsourcing project?

1.2 Stakeholder Register: Desktop Outsourcing

41. How will reports be created?

42. Who is managing stakeholder engagement?

43. What & Why?

44. How big is the gap?

45. What opportunities exist to provide communications?

46. How should employers make voices heard?

47. How much influence do they have on the Desktop Outsourcing project?

48. Who wants to talk about Security?

49. Is your organization ready for change?

50. What are the major Desktop Outsourcing project milestones requiring communications or providing communications opportunities?

51. Who are the stakeholders?

52. What is the power of the stakeholder?

1.3 Stakeholder Analysis Matrix: Desktop Outsourcing

53. How much do resources cost?

54. Location and geographical?

55. How can you counter negative efforts?

56. What actions can be taken to reduce or mitigate risk?

57. Lack of competitive strength?

58. Technology development and innovation?

59. Environmental effects?

60. Participatory approach: how will key stakeholders participate in the Desktop Outsourcing project?

61. What tools would help you communicate?

62. Cultural, attitudinal, behavioural?

63. Philosophy and values?

64. Organizational Applicability?

65. What are the key services, contractual arrangements, or other relationships between stakeholder groups?

66. What are the opportunities for communication?

67. Partnership opportunities/synergies?

68. Who has been involved in the area (thematic or geographic) in the past?

69. Who will be affected by the work?

70. Guiding question: who shall you involve in the making of the stakeholder map?

71. Is there evidence that demonstrates the impact of education on the Desktop Outsourcing projects outcomes?

72. How do customers express needs?

2.0 Planning Process Group: Desktop Outsourcing

73. How can you make your needs known?

74. To what extent are the participating departments coordinating with each other?

75. What should you do next?

76. To what extent has the intervention strategy been adapted to the areas of intervention in which it is being implemented?

77. Is the pace of implementing the products of the program ensuring the completeness of the results of the Desktop Outsourcing project?

78. You are creating your WBS and find that you keep decomposing tasks into smaller and smaller units. How can you tell when you are done?

79. To what extent are the visions and actions of the partners consistent or divergent with regard to the program?

80. How well do the team follow the chosen processes?

81. Desktop Outsourcing project assessment; why did you do this Desktop Outsourcing project?

82. Is the Desktop Outsourcing project making

progress in helping to achieve the set results?

83. First of all, should any action be taken?

84. Will you be replaced?

85. To what extent have public/private national resources and/or counterparts been mobilized to contribute to the programs objective and produce results and impacts?

86. What factors are contributing to progress or delay in the achievement of products and results?

87. Are the necessary foundations in place to ensure the sustainability of the results of the Desktop Outsourcing project?

88. Just how important is your work to the overall success of the Desktop Outsourcing project?

89. How well will the chosen processes produce the expected results?

90. If task x starts two days late, what is the effect on the Desktop Outsourcing project end date?

91. How does activity resource estimation affect activity duration estimation?

92. How many days can task X be late in starting without affecting the Desktop Outsourcing project completion date?

2.1 Project Management Plan: Desktop Outsourcing

93. Why Change?

94. What would you do differently what did not work?

95. What did not work so well?

96. What would you do differently?

97. Was the peer (technical) review of the cost estimates duly coordinated with the cost estimate center of expertise and addressed in the review documentation and certification?

98. What is the business need?

99. Does the implementation plan have an appropriate division of responsibilities?

100. What went wrong?

101. Development trends and opportunities. What if the positive direction and vision of your organization causes expected trends to change?

102. Is the budget realistic?

103. Where does all this information come from?

104. How do you manage integration?

105. Are the existing and future without-plan conditions reasonable and appropriate?

106. What should you drop in order to add something new?

107. Are there any client staffing expectations?

108. Is mitigation authorized or recommended?

109. Are calculations and results of analyzes essentially correct?

110. Does the selected plan protect privacy?

2.2 Scope Management Plan: Desktop Outsourcing

111. Without-plan conditions?

112. Is stakeholder involvement adequate?

113. Are written status reports provided on a designated frequent basis?

114. Have all involved Desktop Outsourcing project stakeholders and work groups committed to the Desktop Outsourcing project?

115. How do you know when you are finished?

116. Is each item clearly and completely defined?

117. Is there general agreement & acceptance of the current status and progress of the Desktop Outsourcing project?

118. What threats might prevent you from getting there?

119. Has a capability assessment been conducted?

120. Are updated Desktop Outsourcing project time & resource estimates reasonable based on the current Desktop Outsourcing project stage?

121. Have the procedures for identifying variances from estimates & adjusting the detailed work program

been followed?

122. Do you secure formal approval of changes and requirements from stakeholders?

123. Is there an on-going process in place to monitor Desktop Outsourcing project risks?

124. Are trade-offs between accepting the risk and mitigating the risk identified?

125. Are corrective actions and variances reported?

126. Are the proposed Desktop Outsourcing project purposes different than the previously authorized Desktop Outsourcing project?

127. Timeline and milestones?

128. Pop quiz – which are the same inputs as in scope planning?

129. Has a quality assurance plan been developed for the Desktop Outsourcing project?

2.3 Requirements Management Plan: Desktop Outsourcing

130. How will the information be distributed?

131. What information regarding the Desktop Outsourcing project requirements will be reported?

132. Do you really need to write this document at all?

133. Is any organizational data being used or stored?

134. Who will approve the requirements (and if multiple approvers, in what order)?

135. Are actual resources expenditures versus planned expenditures acceptable?

136. How will unresolved questions be handled once approval has been obtained?

137. Will you document changes to requirements?

138. When and how will a requirements baseline be established in this Desktop Outsourcing project?

139. Describe the process for rejecting the Desktop Outsourcing project requirements. Who has the authority to reject Desktop Outsourcing project requirements?

140. Who will initially review the Desktop Outsourcing project work or products to ensure it meets the

applicable acceptance criteria?

141. Which hardware or software, related to, or as outcome of the Desktop Outsourcing project is new to your organization?

142. Who came up with this requirement?

143. Will you use an assessment of the Desktop Outsourcing project environment as a tool to discover risk to the requirements process?

144. Have stakeholders been instructed in the Change Control process?

145. Could inaccurate or incomplete requirements in this Desktop Outsourcing project create a serious risk for the business?

146. Who will finally present the work or product(s) for acceptance?

147. Did you distinguish the scope of work the contractor(s) will be required to do?

148. Did you provide clear and concise specifications?

149. Is there formal agreement on who has authority to request a change in requirements?

2.4 Requirements Documentation: Desktop Outsourcing

150. Is the requirement realistically testable?

151. Are there legal issues?

152. Can you check system requirements?

153. What are the attributes of a customer?

154. What is the risk associated with the technology?

155. Are all functions required by the customer included?

156. Does the system provide the functions which best support the customers needs?

157. What if the system wasn t implemented?

158. Where are business rules being captured?

159. Who is involved?

160. How will requirements be documented and who signs off on them?

161. What can tools do for us?

162. Consistency. are there any requirements conflicts?

163. Who is interacting with the system?

164. What will be the integration problems?

165. How do you know when a Requirement is accurate enough?

166. What are the acceptance criteria?

167. Has requirements gathering uncovered information that would necessitate changes?

168. The problem with gathering requirements is right there in the word gathering. What images does it conjure?

2.5 Requirements Traceability Matrix: Desktop Outsourcing

169. Why do you manage scope?

170. Will you use a Requirements Traceability Matrix?

171. Why use a WBS?

172. What is the WBS?

173. What percentage of Desktop Outsourcing projects are producing traceability matrices between requirements and other work products?

174. Describe the process for approving requirements so they can be added to the traceability matrix and Desktop Outsourcing project work can be performed. Will the Desktop Outsourcing project requirements become approved in writing?

175. What are the chronologies, contingencies, consequences, criteria?

176. How do you manage scope?

177. How will it affect the stakeholders personally in career?

178. Do you have a clear understanding of all subcontracts in place?

179. How small is small enough?

180. Is there a requirements traceability process in place?

2.6 Project Scope Statement: Desktop Outsourcing

181. Any new risks introduced or old risks impacted. Are there issues that could affect the existing requirements for the result, service, or product if the scope changes?

182. Who will you recommend approve the change, and when do you recommend the change reviews occur?

183. Relevant - ask yourself can you get there; why are you doing this Desktop Outsourcing project?

184. Are there issues that could affect the existing requirements for the result, service, or product if the scope changes?

185. Will there be a Change Control Process in place?

186. Is the Desktop Outsourcing project sponsor function identified and defined?

187. Are there backup strategies for key members of the Desktop Outsourcing project?

188. Is your organization structure appropriate for the Desktop Outsourcing projects size and complexity?

189. Has the Desktop Outsourcing project scope statement been reviewed as part of the baseline process?

190. Have the reports to be produced, distributed, and filed been defined?

191. Is the scope of your Desktop Outsourcing project well defined?

192. Did your Desktop Outsourcing project ask for this?

193. Will this process be communicated to the customer and Desktop Outsourcing project team?

194. Will the qa related information be reported regularly as part of the status reporting mechanisms?

195. What is a process you might recommend to verify the accuracy of the research deliverable?

196. Were potential customers involved early in the planning process?

197. Is the plan for Desktop Outsourcing project resources adequate?

198. How often do you estimate that the scope might change, and why?

199. Once its defined, what is the stability of the Desktop Outsourcing project scope?

2.7 Assumption and Constraint Log: Desktop Outsourcing

200. Are there unnecessary steps that are creating bottlenecks and/or causing people to wait?

201. Was the document/deliverable developed per the appropriate or required standards (for example, Institute of Electrical and Electronics Engineers standards)?

202. Have you eliminated all duplicative tasks or manual efforts, where appropriate?

203. Have all necessary approvals been obtained?

204. No superfluous information or marketing narrative?

205. What does an audit system look like?

206. Diagrams and tables are included to account for complex concepts and increase overall readability?

207. Are there standards for code development?

208. Is there adequate stakeholder participation for the vetting of requirements definition, changes and management?

209. If it is out of compliance, should the process be amended or should the Plan be amended?

210. Is the definition of the Desktop Outsourcing project scope clear; what needs to be accomplished?

211. What strengths do you have?

212. Does the traceability documentation describe the tool and/or mechanism to be used to capture traceability throughout the life cycle?

213. Have the scope, objectives, costs, benefits and impacts been communicated to all involved and/or impacted stakeholders and work groups?

214. Can you perform this task or activity in a more effective manner?

215. What is positive about the current process?

216. Are formal code reviews conducted?

217. How can constraints be violated?

218. Does the document/deliverable meet all requirements (for example, statement of work) specific to this deliverable?

2.8 Work Breakdown Structure: Desktop Outsourcing

219. How many levels?

220. When does it have to be done?

221. Where does it take place?

222. How will you and your Desktop Outsourcing project team define the Desktop Outsourcing projects scope and work breakdown structure?

223. Is it still viable?

224. What has to be done?

225. Who has to do it?

226. Is it a change in scope?

227. How big is a work-package?

228. Do you need another level?

229. Why is it useful?

230. What is the probability that the Desktop Outsourcing project duration will exceed xx weeks?

231. How much detail?

232. Why would you develop a Work Breakdown

Structure?

233. What is the probability of completing the Desktop Outsourcing project in less that xx days?

234. How far down?

235. When do you stop?

2.9 WBS Dictionary: Desktop Outsourcing

236. Are indirect costs charged to the appropriate indirect pools and incurring organization?

237. Are the wbs and organizational levels for application of the Desktop Outsourcing projected overhead costs identified?

238. Are procedures established to prevent changes to the contract budget base other than the already stated authorized by contractual action?

239. All cwbs elements specified for external reporting?

240. Are current work performance indicators and goals relatable to original goals as modified by contractual changes, replanning, and reprogramming actions?

241. What is the end result of a work package?

242. Are meaningful indicators identified for use in measuring the status of cost and schedule performance?

243. Are detailed work packages planned as far in advance as practicable?

244. Cwbs elements to be subcontracted, with identification of subcontractors?

245. Are all authorized tasks assigned to identified organizational elements?

246. Appropriate work authorization documents which subdivide the contractual effort and responsibilities, within functional organizations?

247. Are overhead budgets and costs being handled according to the disclosure statement when applicable, or otherwise properly classified (for example, engineering overhead, IR&D)?

248. Are the latest revised estimates of costs at completion compared with the established budgets at appropriate levels and causes of variances identified?

249. Are time-phased budgets established for planning and control of level of effort activity by category of resource; for example, type of manpower and/or material?

250. Are Desktop Outsourcing projected overhead costs in each pool and the associated direct costs used as the basis for establishing interim rates for allocating overhead to contracts?

251. Does the cost accumulation system provide for summarization of indirect costs from the point of allocation to the contract total?

252. Should you have a test for each code module?

253. Are data elements reconcilable between internal summary reports and reports forwarded to us?

254. Are significant decision points, constraints, and interfaces identified as key milestones?

2.10 Schedule Management Plan: Desktop Outsourcing

255. Have the procedures for identifying budget variances been followed?

256. Are enough systems & user personnel assigned to the Desktop Outsourcing project?

257. Is there a set of procedures defining the scope, procedures, and deliverables defining quality control?

258. Has the Desktop Outsourcing project manager been identified?

259. Are all payments made according to the contract(s)?

260. Will rolling way planning be used?

261. Are all activities captured and do they address all approved work scope in the Desktop Outsourcing project baseline?

262. Have all documents been archived in a Desktop Outsourcing project repository for each release?

263. Have external dependencies been captured in the schedule?

264. Has a provision been made to reassess Desktop Outsourcing project risks at various Desktop Outsourcing project stages?

265. Perform reality checks on schedules – are all tasks included?

266. Does the Desktop Outsourcing project have a formal Desktop Outsourcing project Charter?

267. Are issues raised, assessed, actioned, and resolved in a timely and efficient manner?

268. Has a structured approach been used to break work effort into manageable components (WBS)?

269. Has a quality assurance plan been developed for the Desktop Outsourcing project?

270. Are target dates established for each milestone deliverable?

271. Is there a formal set of procedures supporting Issues Management?

272. Are all attributes of the activities defined, including risk and uncertainty?

273. Is there a formal process for updating the Desktop Outsourcing project baseline?

274. Are all resource assumptions documented?

2.11 Activity List: Desktop Outsourcing

275. The wbs is developed as part of a joint planning session. and how do you know that youhave done this right?

276. Where will it be performed?

277. Can you determine the activity that must finish, before this activity can start?

278. What is your organizations history in doing similar activities?

279. How will it be performed?

280. When will the work be performed?

281. How should ongoing costs be monitored to try to keep the Desktop Outsourcing project within budget?

282. What will be performed?

283. Are the required resources available or need to be acquired?

284. How can the Desktop Outsourcing project be displayed graphically to better visualize the activities?

285. What is the LF and LS for each activity?

286. What are the critical bottleneck activities?

287. For other activities, how much delay can be tolerated?

288. How do you determine the late start (LS) for each activity?

289. What is the total time required to complete the Desktop Outsourcing project if no delays occur?

290. In what sequence?

291. What are you counting on?

292. How much slack is available in the Desktop Outsourcing project?

293. When do the individual activities need to start and finish?

294. How detailed should a Desktop Outsourcing project get?

2.12 Activity Attributes: Desktop Outsourcing

295. Activity: fair or not fair?

296. What activity do you think you should spend the most time on?

297. Why?

298. How much activity detail is required?

299. Can you re-assign any activities to another resource to resolve an over-allocation?

300. What is the general pattern here?

301. Has management defined a definite timeframe for the turnaround or Desktop Outsourcing project window?

302. Would you consider either of corresponding activities an outlier?

303. How do you manage time?

304. Which method produces the more accurate cost assignment?

305. Were there other ways you could have organized the data to achieve similar results?

306. Is there a trend during the year?

307. Do you feel very comfortable with your prediction?

308. How many days do you need to complete the work scope with a limit of X number of resources?

309. How many resources do you need to complete the work scope within a limit of X number of days?

310. What is missing?

311. Activity: what is In the Bag?

312. Have you identified the Activity Leveling Priority code value on each activity?

2.13 Milestone List: Desktop Outsourcing

313. How late can each activity be finished and started?

314. Level of the Innovation?

315. New USPs?

316. How difficult will it be to do specific activities on this Desktop Outsourcing project?

317. Insurmountable weaknesses?

318. When will the Desktop Outsourcing project be complete?

319. Gaps in capabilities?

320. Sustainable financial backing?

321. Competitive advantages?

322. Usps (unique selling points)?

323. Milestone pages should display the UserID of the person who added the milestone. Does a report or query exist that provides this audit information?

324. How late can the activity finish?

325. Loss of key staff?

326. Effects on core activities, distraction?

327. What specific improvements did you make to the Desktop Outsourcing project proposal since the previous time?

328. How soon can the activity start?

329. What background experience, skills, and strengths does the team bring to your organization?

2.14 Network Diagram: Desktop Outsourcing

330. Review the logical flow of the network diagram. Take a look at which activities you have first and then sequence the activities. Do they make sense?

331. What is the probability of completing the Desktop Outsourcing project in less that xx days?

332. What can be done concurrently?

333. What activities must occur simultaneously with this activity?

334. What job or jobs precede it?

335. What activities must follow this activity?

336. What controls the start and finish of a job?

337. Will crashing x weeks return more in benefits than it costs?

338. Planning: who, how long, what to do?

339. Can you calculate the confidence level?

340. What are the tools?

341. What must be completed before an activity can be started?

342. Are you on time?

343. Where do schedules come from?

344. Are the gantt chart and/or network diagram updated periodically and used to assess the overall Desktop Outsourcing project timetable?

345. What are the Key Success Factors?

346. What job or jobs could run concurrently?

347. What is the completion time?

2.15 Activity Resource Requirements: Desktop Outsourcing

348. When does monitoring begin?

349. Is there anything planned that does not need to be here?

350. What is the Work Plan Standard?

351. Time for overtime?

352. How many signatures do you require on a check and does this match what is in your policy and procedures?

353. Other support in specific areas?

354. Anything else?

355. Are there unresolved issues that need to be addressed?

356. Do you use tools like decomposition and rolling-wave planning to produce the activity list and other outputs?

357. Why do you do that?

358. Which logical relationship does the PDM use most often?

359. What are constraints that you might find during

the Human Resource Planning process?

360. How do you handle petty cash?

2.16 Resource Breakdown Structure: Desktop Outsourcing

361. Why is this important?

362. Who is allowed to perform which functions?

363. How should the information be delivered?

364. Who needs what information?

365. Why time management?

366. When do they need the information?

367. Goals for the Desktop Outsourcing project. What is each stakeholders desired outcome for the Desktop Outsourcing project?

368. Is predictive resource analysis being done?

369. Who will use the system?

370. Who delivers the information?

371. What are the requirements for resource data?

372. Any changes from stakeholders?

373. The list could probably go on, but, the thing that you would most like to know is, How long & How much?

374. What defines a successful Desktop Outsourcing project?

375. What is the difference between % Complete and % work?

376. What defines a successful Desktop Outsourcing project?

377. Which resource planning tool provides information on resource responsibility and accountability?

378. How can this help you with team building?

2.17 Activity Duration Estimates: Desktop Outsourcing

379. Is earned value analysis completed to assess Desktop Outsourcing project performance?

380. Which types of reports would help provide summary information to senior management?

381. What time management activity should you do NEXT?

382. Are activity dependencies documented?

383. (Cpi), and schedule performance index (spi) for the Desktop Outsourcing project?

384. Are training needs identified when resources do not have the required skills to complete Desktop Outsourcing project activities?

385. Are procurement documents used to solicit accurate and complete proposals from prospective sellers?

386. How do you enter durations, link tasks, and view critical path information?

387. What type of people would you want on your team?

388. What do corresponding sources say about Desktop Outsourcing project management?

389. What is wrong with this scenario?

390. How difficult will it be to complete specific activities on this Desktop Outsourcing project?

391. Are changes to the scope managed according to defined procedures?

392. Is risk identification completed regularly throughout the Desktop Outsourcing project?

393. What are the largest companies that provide information technology outsourcing services?

394. What are the main processes included in Desktop Outsourcing project quality management?

395. What type of information goes in a quality assurance plan?

396. Which frame seemed to be the most important and why?

2.18 Duration Estimating Worksheet: Desktop Outsourcing

397. When does your organization expect to be able to complete it?

398. Value pocket identification & quantification what are value pockets?

399. What is an Average Desktop Outsourcing project?

400. What info is needed?

401. What work will be included in the Desktop Outsourcing project?

402. How should ongoing costs be monitored to try to keep the Desktop Outsourcing project within budget?

403. What is your role?

404. Does the Desktop Outsourcing project provide innovative ways for stakeholders to overcome obstacles or deliver better outcomes?

405. What went right?

406. When, then?

407. Science = process: remember the scientific method?

408. Do any colleagues have experience with your

organization and/or RFPs?

409. What questions do you have?

410. Why estimate time and cost?

411. What is next?

412. Why estimate costs?

413. Is the Desktop Outsourcing project responsive to community need?

414. Done before proceeding with this activity or what can be done concurrently?

2.19 Project Schedule: Desktop Outsourcing

415. To what degree is do you feel the entire team was committed to the Desktop Outsourcing project schedule?

416. Are all remaining durations correct?

417. Should you include sub-activities?

418. What is Desktop Outsourcing project management?

419. Why do you think schedule issues often cause the most conflicts on Desktop Outsourcing projects?

420. How can you fix it?

421. What is the difference?

422. How do you use schedules?

423. Month Desktop Outsourcing project take?

424. Meet requirements?

425. Why do you need to manage Desktop Outsourcing project Risk?

426. Is the structure for tracking the Desktop Outsourcing project schedule well defined and assigned to a specific individual?

427. What does that mean?

428. Is infrastructure setup part of your Desktop Outsourcing project?

429. How can you minimize or control changes to Desktop Outsourcing project schedules?

430. How much slack is available in the Desktop Outsourcing project?

431. Does the condition or event threaten the Desktop Outsourcing projects objectives in any ways?

432. Why or why not?

2.20 Cost Management Plan: Desktop Outsourcing

433. Are mitigation strategies identified?

434. Eac -estimate at completion, what is the total job expected to cost?

435. Are all vendor contracts closed out?

436. Is current scope of the Desktop Outsourcing project substantially different than that originally defined?

437. Has a quality assurance plan been developed for the Desktop Outsourcing project?

438. Is quality monitored from the perspective of the customers needs and expectations?

439. Will the earned value reporting interface between time and cost management?

440. Are action items captured and managed?

441. Are the key elements of a Desktop Outsourcing project Charter present?

442. Are assumptions being identified, recorded, analyzed, qualified and closed?

443. Have stakeholder accountabilities & responsibilities been clearly defined?

444. Schedule preparation – how will the schedules be prepared during each phase of the Desktop Outsourcing project?

445. Who will prepare the cost estimates?

446. Has a resource management plan been created?

447. Is a stakeholder management plan in place that covers topics?

448. Have Desktop Outsourcing project management standards and procedures been identified / established and documented?

449. Does the detailed work plan match the complexity of tasks with the capabilities of personnel?

450. Has a Desktop Outsourcing project Communications Plan been developed?

451. Outside experts?

2.21 Activity Cost Estimates: Desktop Outsourcing

452. The impact and what actions were taken?

453. What procedures are put in place regarding bidding and cost comparisons, if any?

454. Padding is bad and contingencies are good. what is the difference?

455. What communication items need improvement?

456. Was the consultant knowledgeable about the program?

457. Can you change your activities?

458. What areas were overlooked on this Desktop Outsourcing project?

459. Does the activity serve a common type of customer?

460. How do you fund change orders?

461. How do you do activity recasts?

462. In which phase of the acquisition process cycle does source qualifications reside?

463. Maintenance Reserve?

464. Where can you get activity reports?

465. What is Desktop Outsourcing project cost management?

466. Does the estimator estimate by task or by person?

467. What happens if you cannot produce the documentation for the single audit?

468. Were sponsors and decision makers available when needed outside regularly scheduled meetings?

2.22 Cost Estimating Worksheet: Desktop Outsourcing

469. Does the Desktop Outsourcing project provide innovative ways for stakeholders to overcome obstacles or deliver better outcomes?

470. Is the Desktop Outsourcing project responsive to community need?

471. What is the purpose of estimating?

472. What will others want?

473. Ask: are others positioned to know, are others credible, and will others cooperate?

474. Is it feasible to establish a control group arrangement?

475. Will the Desktop Outsourcing project collaborate with the local community and leverage resources?

476. What costs are to be estimated?

477. Can a trend be established from historical performance data on the selected measure and are the criteria for using trend analysis or forecasting methods met?

478. What additional Desktop Outsourcing project(s) could be initiated as a result of this Desktop Outsourcing project?

479. Identify the timeframe necessary to monitor progress and collect data to determine how the selected measure has changed?

480. How will the results be shared and to whom?

481. What is the estimated labor cost today based upon this information?

482. What happens to any remaining funds not used?

483. What can be included?

484. Who is best positioned to know and assist in identifying corresponding factors?

2.23 Cost Baseline: Desktop Outsourcing

485. What does a good WBS NOT look like?

486. Escalation criteria met?

487. Are procedures defined by which the cost baseline may be changed?

488. How accurate do cost estimates need to be?

489. Have all approved changes to the Desktop Outsourcing project requirement been identified and impact on the performance, cost, and schedule baselines documented?

490. How likely is it to go wrong?

491. Have all approved changes to the cost baseline been identified and impact on the Desktop Outsourcing project documented?

492. At which frequency ?

493. Is the requested change request a result of changes in other Desktop Outsourcing project(s)?

494. Has training and knowledge transfer of the operations organization been completed?

495. Have you identified skills that are missing from your team?

496. Does the suggested change request represent a desired enhancement to the products functionality?

497. Is request in line with priorities?

498. Impact to environment?

499. Who will use corresponding metrics ?

500. When should cost estimates be developed?

501. On budget?

502. Has the appropriate access to relevant data and analysis capability been granted?

503. What is the consequence?

504. Are there contingencies or conditions related to the acceptance?

2.24 Quality Management Plan: Desktop Outsourcing

505. Who do you send data to?

506. What would you gain if you spent time working to improve this process?

507. How does your organization ensure the quality, reliability, and user-friendliness of its hardware and software?

508. After observing execution of process, is it in compliance with the documented Plan?

509. Methodology followed?

510. How are changes to procedures made?

511. How are calibration records kept?

512. How do you measure?

513. Written by multiple authors and in multiple writing styles?

514. Does the program use other agents to collect samples?

515. How are changes approved?

516. How do senior leaders create and communicate values and performance expectations?

517. How does your organization maintain a safe and healthy work environment?

518. What has the QM Collaboration done?

519. How is staff informed of proper reporting methods?

520. Who is responsible?

521. How does the material compare to a regulatory threshold?

522. What are your organizations key processes (product, service, business, and support)?

523. Are there processes in place to ensure internal consistency between the source code components?

2.25 Quality Metrics: Desktop Outsourcing

524. Should a modifier be included?

525. How are requirements conflicts resolved?

526. Which are the right metrics to use?

527. Is quality culture a competitive advantage?

528. Why is now the time for quality metrics?

529. What happens if you get an abnormal result?

530. Do you stratify metrics by product or site?

531. Subjective quality component: customer satisfaction, how do you measure it?

532. Where is quality now?

533. What percentage are outcome-based?

534. How does one achieve stability?

535. What is the benchmark?

536. Filter visualizations of interest?

537. Is material complete (and does it meet the standards)?

538. What about still open problems?

539. What metrics are important and most beneficial to measure?

540. What forces exist that would cause them to change?

541. When will the Final Guidance will be issued?

542. Are there already quality metrics available that detect nonlinear embeddings and trends similar to the users perception?

543. What if the biggest risk to your business were the already stated people who do not complain?

2.26 Process Improvement Plan: Desktop Outsourcing

544. Have the supporting tools been developed or acquired?

545. What actions are needed to address the problems and achieve the goals?

546. The motive is determined by asking, Why do you want to achieve this goal?

547. Where do you focus?

548. If a process improvement framework is being used, which elements will help the problems and goals listed?

549. Has a process guide to collect the data been developed?

550. Are there forms and procedures to collect and record the data?

551. What is the return on investment?

552. What makes people good SPI coaches?

553. Have the frequency of collection and the points in the process where measurements will be made been determined?

554. Are you making progress on the goals?

555. Are you meeting the quality standards?

556. Where do you want to be?

557. What lessons have you learned so far?

558. Why do you want to achieve the goal?

559. What is the test-cycle concept?

560. Have storage and access mechanisms and procedures been determined?

561. Who should prepare the process improvement action plan?

562. What personnel are the coaches for your initiative?

2.27 Responsibility Assignment Matrix: Desktop Outsourcing

563. Does a missing responsibility indicate that the current Desktop Outsourcing project is not yet fully understood?

564. Too many is: do all the identified roles need to be routinely informed or only in exceptional circumstances?

565. Past experience – the person or the group worked at something similar in the past?

566. Changes in the nature of the overhead requirements?

567. What do people write/say on status/Desktop Outsourcing project reports?

568. Are estimates of costs at completion generated in a rational, consistent manner?

569. Are there any drawbacks to using a responsibility assignment matrix?

570. Are management actions taken to reduce indirect costs when there are significant adverse variances?

571. Are data elements reconcilable between internal summary reports and reports forwarded to stakeholders?

572. Too many rs: with too many people labeled as doing the work, are there too many hands involved?

573. How do you manage human resources?

574. Is accountability placed at the lowest-possible level within the Desktop Outsourcing project so that decisions can be made at that level?

575. What travel needed?

576. Are the wbs and organizational levels for application of the Desktop Outsourcing projected overhead costs identified?

577. Is work progressively subdivided into detailed work packages as requirements are defined?

578. How cost benefit analysis?

579. The anticipated business volume?

580. Are the bases and rates for allocating costs from each indirect pool consistently applied?

581. Not any rs, as, or cs: if an identified role is only informed, should others be eliminated from the matrix?

2.28 Roles and Responsibilities: Desktop Outsourcing

582. Are governance roles and responsibilities documented?

583. What areas would you highlight for changes or improvements?

584. Was the expectation clearly communicated?

585. Are your policies supportive of a culture of quality data?

586. What areas of supervision are challenging for you?

587. Are Desktop Outsourcing project team roles and responsibilities identified and documented?

588. What should you do now to prepare yourself for a promotion, increased responsibilities or a different job?

589. What expectations were NOT met?

590. What should you do now to ensure that you are exceeding expectations and excelling in your current position?

591. Are the quality assurance functions and related roles and responsibilities clearly defined?

592. Be specific; avoid generalities. Thank you and great work alone are insufficient. What exactly do you appreciate and why?

593. Once the responsibilities are defined for the Desktop Outsourcing project, have the deliverables, roles and responsibilities been clearly communicated to every participant?

594. Implementation of actions: Who are the responsible units?

595. Does your vision/mission support a culture of quality data?

596. Is feedback clearly communicated and non-judgmental?

597. What should you highlight for improvement?

598. What expectations were met?

599. Are your budgets supportive of a culture of quality data?

600. Where are you most strong as a supervisor?

2.29 Human Resource Management Plan: Desktop Outsourcing

601. Are internal Desktop Outsourcing project status meetings held at reasonable intervals?

602. What were things that you did very well and want to do the same again on the next Desktop Outsourcing project?

603. Have the key elements of a coherent Desktop Outsourcing project management strategy been established?

604. Are software metrics formally captured, analyzed and used as a basis for other Desktop Outsourcing project estimates?

605. Is the structure for tracking the Desktop Outsourcing project schedule well defined and assigned to a specific individual?

606. Was the scope definition used in task sequencing?

607. What is the boss?

608. Have process improvement efforts been completed before requirements efforts begin?

609. Are Desktop Outsourcing project team members committed fulltime?

610. What areas were overlooked on this Desktop Outsourcing project?

611. Are updated Desktop Outsourcing project time & resource estimates reasonable based on the current Desktop Outsourcing project stage?

612. Have adequate resources been provided by management to ensure Desktop Outsourcing project success?

613. Is it possible to track all classes of Desktop Outsourcing project work (e.g. scheduled, unscheduled, defect repair, etc.)?

614. Is there an approved case?

615. How will the Desktop Outsourcing project manage expectations & meet needs and requirements?

616. Is Desktop Outsourcing project work proceeding in accordance with the original Desktop Outsourcing project schedule?

617. Is there an onboarding process in place?

2.30 Communications Management Plan: Desktop Outsourcing

618. Which team member will work with each stakeholder?

619. What data is going to be required?

620. In your work, how much time is spent on stakeholder identification?

621. How will the person responsible for executing the communication item be notified?

622. How often do you engage with stakeholders?

623. Who are the members of the governing body?

624. Who is the stakeholder?

625. How much time does it take to do it?

626. Who did you turn to if you had questions?

627. Who will use or be affected by the result of a Desktop Outsourcing project?

628. Who to share with?

629. How did the term stakeholder originate?

630. How were corresponding initiatives successful?

631. How is this initiative related to other portfolios, programs, or Desktop Outsourcing projects?

632. Are there potential barriers between the team and the stakeholder?

633. Who have you worked with in past, similar initiatives?

634. What is the political influence?

635. Why manage stakeholders?

636. Do you then often overlook a key stakeholder or stakeholder group?

2.31 Risk Management Plan: Desktop Outsourcing

637. Risk categories: what are the main categories of risks that should be addressed on this Desktop Outsourcing project?

638. How is the audit profession changing?

639. Why do you want risk management?

640. Do the requirements require the creation of components that are unlike anything your organization has previously built?

641. Is the customer willing to establish rapid communication links with the developer?

642. Do end-users have realistic expectations?

643. My Desktop Outsourcing project leader has suddenly left your organization, what do you do?

644. How risk averse are you?

645. How will the Desktop Outsourcing project know if your organizations risk response actions were effective?

646. Are requirements fully understood by the software engineering team and customers?

647. Do requirements demand the use of new

analysis, design, or testing methods?

648. Does the Desktop Outsourcing project team have experience with the technology to be implemented?

649. User involvement: do you have the right users?

650. Workarounds are determined during which step of risk management?

651. Risk documentation: what reporting formats and processes will be used for risk management activities?

652. If you can not fix it, how do you do it differently?

653. Is the customer willing to participate in reviews?

654. Are the metrics meaningful and useful?

655. How is risk response planning performed?

2.32 Risk Register: Desktop Outsourcing

656. What is the probability and impact of the risk occurring?

657. What are your key risks/show istoppers and what is being done to manage them?

658. Assume the risk event or situation happens, what would the impact be?

659. What can be done about it?

660. Are there any gaps in the evidence?

661. What should you do now?

662. Can the likelihood and impact of failing to achieve corresponding recommendations and action plans be assessed?

663. How could corresponding Risk affect the Desktop Outsourcing project in terms of cost and schedule?

664. What could prevent you delivering on the strategic program objectives and what is being done to mitigate corresponding issues?

665. Are there any knock-on effects/impact on any of the other areas?

666. What are the main aims, objectives of the policy,

strategy, or service and the intended outcomes?

667. Are corrective measures implemented as planned?

668. Budget and schedule: what are the estimated costs and schedules for performing risk-related activities?

669. Why would you develop a risk register?

670. How are risks identified?

671. People risk -are people with appropriate skills available to help complete the Desktop Outsourcing project?

672. Market risk -will the new service or product be useful to your organization or marketable to others?

2.33 Probability and Impact Assessment: Desktop Outsourcing

673. Have decisions that should be left open because of inadequate information on technology been identified and responsibility assigned for reducing the uncertainty?

674. How do risks change during the Desktop Outsourcing projects life cycle?

675. What are the industrial relations prevailing in your organization?

676. Are testing tools available and suitable?

677. How do risks change during a Desktop Outsourcing project life cycle?

678. What are the tools and techniques used in managing the challenges faced?

679. Do you train all developers in the process?

680. What is the risk appetite?

681. Are the risk data complete?

682. What will be the likely political environment during the life of the Desktop Outsourcing project?

683. What are the chances the event will occur?

684. What risks does your organization have if the Desktop Outsourcing projects fail to meet deadline?

685. What action do you usually take against risks?

686. Who will be responsible for a slippage?

687. What is the likelihood?

688. Are there new risks that mitigation strategies might introduce?

689. How realistic is the timing of introduction?

690. What are the current demands of the customer?

691. How carefully have the potential competitors been identified?

2.34 Probability and Impact Matrix: Desktop Outsourcing

692. Are tools for analysis and design available?

693. What would be the best solution?

694. What are the probable external agencies to act as Desktop Outsourcing project manager?

695. Who should be notified of the occurrence of each of the risk indicators?

696. Workarounds are determined during which risk management process?

697. What will the damage be?

698. What are the levels of understanding of the future users of this technology?

699. What is the political situation at present?

700. Should the risk be taken at all?

701. What action would you take to the identified risks in the Desktop Outsourcing project?

702. What kind of preparation would be required to do this?

703. What things are likely to change?

704. What will be the likely political situation during the life of the Desktop Outsourcing project?

705. What are the current or emerging trends of culture?

706. Are formal technical reviews part of this process?

707. What is Desktop Outsourcing project risk management?

708. Has something like this been done before?

2.35 Risk Data Sheet: Desktop Outsourcing

709. What are the main opportunities available to you that you should grab while you can?

710. Is the data sufficiently specified in terms of the type of failure being analyzed, and its frequency or probability?

711. How do you handle product safely?

712. How can it happen?

713. What can you do?

714. What was measured?

715. Risk of what?

716. What are the main threats to your existence?

717. Has a sensitivity analysis been carried out?

718. Are new hazards created?

719. What is the environment within which you operate (social trends, economic, community values, broad based participation, national directions etc.)?

720. Type of risk identified?

721. What will be the consequences if the risk

happens?

722. What were the Causes that contributed?

723. What actions can be taken to eliminate or remove risk?

724. What can happen?

725. How reliable is the data source?

726. What are you trying to achieve (Objectives)?

727. What are your core values?

728. What will be the consequences if it happens?

2.36 Procurement Management Plan: Desktop Outsourcing

729. Is it possible to track all classes of Desktop Outsourcing project work (e.g. scheduled, unscheduled, defect repair, etc.)?

730. Published materials?

731. Are estimating assumptions and constraints captured?

732. Is there a procurement management plan in place?

733. Are any non-compliance issues that exist communicated to your organization?

734. Are all key components of a Quality Assurance Plan present?

735. Are changes in deliverable commitments agreed to by all affected groups & individuals?

736. Alignment to strategic goals & objectives?

737. How will multiple providers be managed?

738. Have lessons learned been conducted after each Desktop Outsourcing project release?

739. Are Desktop Outsourcing project team members involved in detailed estimating and scheduling?

740. Are metrics used to evaluate and manage Vendors?

741. Are key risk mitigation strategies added to the Desktop Outsourcing project schedule?

742. How and when do you enter into Desktop Outsourcing project Procurement Management?

743. Are changes in scope (deliverable commitments) agreed to by all affected groups & individuals?

744. Does the Desktop Outsourcing project have a formal Desktop Outsourcing project Charter?

745. Have all involved Desktop Outsourcing project stakeholders and work groups committed to the Desktop Outsourcing project?

2.37 Source Selection Criteria: Desktop Outsourcing

746. Are evaluators ready to begin this task?

747. When is it appropriate to issue a Draft Request for Proposal (DRFP)?

748. What does an evaluation address and what does a sample resemble?

749. How will you evaluate offerors proposals?

750. Are types/quantities of material, facilities appropriate?

751. Is experience evaluated?

752. How important is cost in the source selection decision relative to past performance and technical considerations?

753. Is a letter of commitment from each proposed team member and key subcontractor included?

754. What is price analysis and when should it be performed?

755. Have team members been adequately trained?

756. How much weight should be placed on past performance information?

757. How are oral presentations documented?

758. How can business terms and conditions be improved to yield more effective price competition?

759. Is this a cost contract?

760. What benefits are accrued from issuing a DRFP in advance of issuing a final RFP?

761. What are open book debriefings?

762. How should the oral presentations be handled?

763. In the technical/management area, what criteria do you use to determine the final evaluation ratings?

764. Who is entitled to a debriefing?

765. What should a Draft Request for Proposal (DRFP) include?

2.38 Stakeholder Management Plan: Desktop Outsourcing

766. What is to be the method of release?

767. Will Desktop Outsourcing project success require up to date information at a moments notice?

768. Are you meeting your customers expectations consistently?

769. Where will verification occur, and by whom?

770. Are tasks tracked by hours?

771. Has your organization readiness assessment been conducted?

772. Who is accountable for the achievement of the targeted outcome(s) and reports on the progress towards the target?

773. Is there a formal process for updating the Desktop Outsourcing project baseline?

774. Have Desktop Outsourcing project success criteria been defined?

775. Are actuals compared against estimates to analyze and correct variances?

776. Are schedule deliverables actually delivered?

777. Are cause and effect determined for risks when they occur?

778. Are milestone deliverables effectively tracked and compared to Desktop Outsourcing project plan?

779. Do any protocols apply for records management?

780. When would you develop a Desktop Outsourcing project Execution Plan?

2.39 Change Management Plan: Desktop Outsourcing

781. Do you need a new organization structure?

782. What type of materials/channels will be available to leverage?

783. What work practices will be affected?

784. What new behaviours are required?

785. Has a training need analysis been carried out?

786. Is there a support model for this application and are the details available for distribution?

787. What are the specific target groups/audiences that will be impacted by this change?

788. Who might present the most resistance?

789. Who should be involved in developing a change management strategy?

790. How badly can information be misinterpreted?

791. Who might be able to help you the most?

792. What communication network would you use – informal or formal?

793. What risks may occur upfront, during

implementation and after implementation?

794. How will you deal with anger about the restricting of communications due to confidentiality considerations?

795. What skills, education, knowledge, or work experiences should the resources have for each identified competency?

796. What are the current methods of sharing information and do there need to be new ones developed?

797. What does a resilient organization look like?

798. How far reaching in your organization is the change?

799. Is there a software application relevant to this deliverable?

800. How much change management is needed?

3.0 Executing Process Group: Desktop Outsourcing

801. What are the critical steps involved in selecting measures and initiatives?

802. Mitigate. what will you do to minimize the impact should a risk event occur?

803. What does it mean to take a systems view of a Desktop Outsourcing project?

804. What are crucial elements of successful Desktop Outsourcing project plan execution?

805. What are the key components of the Desktop Outsourcing project communications plan?

806. What areas were overlooked on this Desktop Outsourcing project?

807. What are the main types of goods and services being outsourced?

808. How do you control progress of your Desktop Outsourcing project?

809. If a risk event occurs, what will you do?

810. Is the Desktop Outsourcing project making progress in helping to achieve the set results?

811. On which process should team members spend

the most time?

812. Have operating capacities been created and/or reinforced in partners?

813. What is the difference between conceptual, application, and evaluative questions?

814. Are decisions made in a timely manner?

815. Does the Desktop Outsourcing project team have the right skills?

816. What areas does the group agree are the biggest success on the Desktop Outsourcing project?

817. How could you control progress of your Desktop Outsourcing project?

818. How can software assist in procuring goods and services?

819. Is the schedule for the set products being met?

3.1 Team Member Status Report: Desktop Outsourcing

820. How it is to be done?

821. What is to be done?

822. Is there evidence that staff is taking a more professional approach toward management of your organizations Desktop Outsourcing projects?

823. The problem with Reward & Recognition Programs is that the truly deserving people all too often get left out. How can you make it practical?

824. Are your organizations Desktop Outsourcing projects more successful over time?

825. What specific interest groups do you have in place?

826. Does every department have to have a Desktop Outsourcing project Manager on staff?

827. When a teams productivity and success depend on collaboration and the efficient flow of information, what generally fails them?

828. Does your organization have the means (staff, money, contract, etc.) to produce or to acquire the product, good, or service?

829. How will resource planning be done?

830. Will the staff do training or is that done by a third party?

831. Why is it to be done?

832. How can you make it practical?

833. Are the attitudes of staff regarding Desktop Outsourcing project work improving?

834. Are the products of your organizations Desktop Outsourcing projects meeting customers objectives?

835. Do you have an Enterprise Desktop Outsourcing project Management Office (EPMO)?

836. How does this product, good, or service meet the needs of the Desktop Outsourcing project and your organization as a whole?

837. Does the product, good, or service already exist within your organization?

838. How much risk is involved?

3.2 Change Request: Desktop Outsourcing

839. How do you get changes (code) out in a timely manner?

840. Where do changes come from?

841. Should a more thorough impact analysis be conducted?

842. Has your address changed?

843. Are change requests logged and managed?

844. Who will perform the change?

845. What is the change request log?

846. Who is responsible to authorize changes?

847. Will there be a change request form in use?

848. What must be taken into consideration when introducing change control programs?

849. Have scm procedures for noting the change, recording it, and reporting it been followed?

850. How shall the implementation of changes be recorded?

851. Who is included in the change control team?

852. Who needs to approve change requests?

853. What kind of information about the change request needs to be captured?

854. Will new change requests be acknowledged in a timely manner?

855. Have all related configuration items been properly updated?

856. What are the duties of the change control team?

857. Who is responsible for the implementation and monitoring of all measures?

858. Who can suggest changes?

3.3 Change Log: Desktop Outsourcing

859. Is the change request within Desktop Outsourcing project scope?

860. Is the change request open, closed or pending?

861. Will the Desktop Outsourcing project fail if the change request is not executed?

862. Is the submitted change a new change or a modification of a previously approved change?

863. Is the requested change request a result of changes in other Desktop Outsourcing project(s)?

864. When was the request approved?

865. Does the suggested change request seem to represent a necessary enhancement to the product?

866. Is this a mandatory replacement?

867. Do the described changes impact on the integrity or security of the system?

868. Is the change backward compatible without limitations?

869. How does this change affect the timeline of the schedule?

870. When was the request submitted?

871. Who initiated the change request?

872. How does this change affect scope?

873. How does this relate to the standards developed for specific business processes?

3.4 Decision Log: Desktop Outsourcing

874. With whom was the decision shared or considered?

875. It becomes critical to track and periodically revisit both operational effectiveness; Are you noticing all that you need to, and are you interpreting what you see effectively?

876. Is your opponent open to a non-traditional workflow, or will it likely challenge anything you do?

877. Is everything working as expected?

878. What is the average size of your matters in an applicable measurement?

879. What are the cost implications?

880. What eDiscovery problem or issue did your organization set out to fix or make better?

881. Decision-making process; how will the team make decisions?

882. How do you know when you are achieving it?

883. How consolidated and comprehensive a story can you tell by capturing currently available incident data in a central location and through a log of key decisions during an incident?

884. Do strategies and tactics aimed at less than full control reduce the costs of management or simply shift the cost burden?

885. Adversarial environment. is your opponent open to a non-traditional workflow, or will it likely challenge anything you do?

886. What is the line where eDiscovery ends and document review begins?

887. How does the use a Decision Support System influence the strategies/tactics or costs?

888. How does an increasing emphasis on cost containment influence the strategies and tactics used?

889. What was the rationale for the decision?

890. Who will be given a copy of this document and where will it be kept?

891. What is your overall strategy for quality control / quality assurance procedures?

892. How do you define success?

893. At what point in time does loss become unacceptable?

3.5 Quality Audit: Desktop Outsourcing

894. How does your organization know that its staff entrance standards are appropriately effective and constructive and being implemented consistently?

895. Are salvageable and salvaged medical devices stored in a manner to prevent damage and/or contamination?

896. How does the organization know that its system for maintaining and advancing the capabilities of its staff, particularly in relation to the Mission of the organization, is appropriately effective and constructive?

897. Are complaint files maintained?

898. Is quality audit a prerequisite for program accreditation or program recognition?

899. How does your organization know that its staff support services planning and management systems are appropriately effective and constructive?

900. What does an analysis of your organizations staff profile suggest in terms of its planning, and how is this being addressed?

901. Are all complaints involving the possible failure of a device, labeling, or packaging to meet any of its specifications reviewed, evaluated, and investigated?

902. Is the reports overall tone appropriate?

903. How does your organization know that its relationships with the community at large are appropriately effective and constructive?

904. Are all areas associated with the storage and reconditioning of devices clean, free of rubbish, adequately ventilated and in good repair?

905. What has changed/improved as a result of the review processes?

906. How does your organization know that its financial management system is appropriately effective and constructive?

907. Are there appropriate means for intervening if necessary?

908. Have personnel cleanliness and health requirements been established?

909. How does your organization know that its systems for communicating with and among staff are appropriately effective and constructive?

910. Are all records associated with the reconditioning of a device maintained for a minimum of two years after the sale or disposal of the last device within a lot of merchandise?

911. How does your organization know that its information technology system is serving its needs as effectively and constructively as is appropriate?

912. How does your organization know that its public relations and marketing systems are appropriately effective and constructive?

913. Quality is about improvement and accountability. The immediate questions that arise out of that statement are: (i) improvement on what, and (ii) accountable to whom?

3.6 Team Directory: Desktop Outsourcing

914. Process decisions: is work progressing on schedule and per contract requirements?

915. Who are your stakeholders (customers, sponsors, end users, team members)?

916. Who should receive information (all stakeholders)?

917. Decisions: is the most suitable form of contract being used?

918. Where will the product be used and/or delivered or built when appropriate?

919. What are you going to deliver or accomplish?

920. Who will be the stakeholders on your next Desktop Outsourcing project?

921. Process decisions: do invoice amounts match accepted work in place?

922. When will you produce deliverables?

923. Process decisions: are contractors adequately prosecuting the work?

924. How will the team handle changes?

925. Is construction on schedule?

926. Who will write the meeting minutes and distribute?

927. How will you accomplish and manage the objectives?

928. Contract requirements complied with?

929. Who are the Team Members?

930. When does information need to be distributed?

931. How and in what format should information be presented?

932. Why is the work necessary?

3.7 Team Operating Agreement: Desktop Outsourcing

933. What individual strengths does each team member bring to the group?

934. Must your team members rely on the expertise of other members to complete tasks?

935. Why does your organization want to participate in teaming?

936. Do you ensure that all participants know how to use the required technology?

937. Do you listen for voice tone and word choice to understand the meaning behind words?

938. Do you solicit member feedback about meetings and what would make them better?

939. Communication protocols: how will the team communicate?

940. Are there the right people on your team?

941. How do you want to be thought of and known within your organization?

942. Do you send out the agenda and meeting materials in advance?

943. How will group handle unplanned absences?

944. Have you established procedures that team members can follow to work effectively together, such as a team operating agreement?

945. Do you determine the meeting length and time of day?

946. Methodologies: how will key team processes be implemented, such as training, research, work deliverable production, review and approval processes, knowledge management, and meeting procedures?

947. Do you ask participants to close laptops and place mobile devices on silent on the table while the meeting is in progress?

948. What went well?

949. What is your unique contribution to your organization?

950. Did you recap the meeting purpose, time, and expectations?

951. Do you post any action items, due dates, and responsibilities on the team website?

3.8 Team Performance Assessment: Desktop Outsourcing

952. Can familiarity breed backup?

953. What are teams?

954. To what degree can the team ensure that all members are individually and jointly accountable for the teams purpose, goals, approach, and work-products?

955. What do you think is the most constructive thing that could be done now to resolve considerations and disputes about method variance?

956. To what degree do members understand and articulate the same purpose without relying on ambiguous abstractions?

957. To what degree is there a sense that only the team can succeed?

958. How do you recognize and praise members for contributions?

959. How much interpersonal friction is there in your team?

960. If you are worried about method variance before you collect data, what sort of design elements might you include to reduce or eliminate the threat of method variance?

961. To what degree do team members feel that the purpose of the team is important, if not exciting?

962. To what degree will new and supplemental skills be introduced as the need is recognized?

963. Do you give group members authority to make at least some important decisions?

964. To what degree are the teams goals and objectives clear, simple, and measurable?

965. To what degree can team members frequently and easily communicate with one another?

966. To what degree are fresh input and perspectives systematically caught and added (for example, through information and analysis, new members, and senior sponsors)?

967. To what degree will the team ensure that all members equitably share the work essential to the success of the team?

968. Effects of crew composition on crew performance: Does the whole equal the sum of its parts?

969. What are you doing specifically to develop the leaders around you?

970. To what degree do team members articulate the teams work approach?

971. To what degree are corresponding categories of

skills either actually or potentially represented across the membership?

3.9 Team Member Performance Assessment: Desktop Outsourcing

972. How do you determine which data are the most important to use, analyze, or review?

973. What is the Business Management Oversight Process?

974. What specific plans do you have for developing effective cross-platform assessments in a blended learning environment?

975. What evaluation results did you have?

976. To what extent are systems and applications (e.g., game engine, mobile device platform) utilized?

977. What are the key duties or tasks of the Ratee?

978. How does your team work together?

979. What evaluation results do you have?

980. What, if any, steps are available for employees who feel they have been unfairly or inaccurately rated?

981. Is there reluctance to join a team?

982. To what degree do members articulate the goals beyond the team membership?

983. What stakeholders must be involved in the development and oversight of the performance plan?

984. How effective is training that is delivered through technology-based platforms?

985. Does platform-specific assessment information contribute to training placement or tailoring of instruction (e.g. aptitude-treatment interaction)?

986. What makes them effective?

987. What types of learning are targeted (e.g., cognitive, affective, psychomotor, procedural)?

988. To what degree can the team measure progress against specific goals?

989. How often should assessments be conducted?

990. How will they be formed?

991. Where can team members go for more detailed information on performance measurement and assessment?

3.10 Issue Log: Desktop Outsourcing

992. Which stakeholders can influence others?

993. Who reported the issue?

994. What approaches do you use?

995. Is the issue log kept in a safe place?

996. Do you often overlook a key stakeholder or stakeholder group?

997. Who is involved as you identify stakeholders?

998. What help do you and your team need from the stakeholders?

999. What is the impact on the Business Case?

1000. Is access to the Issue Log controlled?

1001. What steps can you take for positive relationships?

1002. Are stakeholder roles recognized by your organization?

1003. Are the stakeholders getting the information they need, are they consulted, are concerns addressed?

1004. Are the Desktop Outsourcing project issues uniquely identified, including to which product they refer?

1005. Who is the issue assigned to?

1006. Can an impact cause deviation beyond team, stage or Desktop Outsourcing project tolerances?

1007. How is this initiative related to other portfolios, programs, or Desktop Outsourcing projects?

1008. What are the stakeholders interrelationships?

1009. Are there too many who have an interest in some aspect of your work?

4.0 Monitoring and Controlling Process Group: Desktop Outsourcing

1010. What areas does the group agree are the biggest success on the Desktop Outsourcing project?

1011. Are there areas that need improvement?

1012. Purpose: toward what end is the evaluation being conducted?

1013. What were things that you need to improve?

1014. Who are the Desktop Outsourcing project stakeholders?

1015. Who needs to be engaged upfront to ensure use of results?

1016. How is agile program management done?

1017. Are the necessary foundations in place to ensure the sustainability of the results of the programme?

1018. What do they need to know about the Desktop Outsourcing project?

1019. Is progress on outcomes due to your program?

1020. Is there undesirable impact on staff or resources?

1021. Based on your Desktop Outsourcing project communication management plan, what worked well?

1022. Overall, how does the program function to serve the clients?

1023. Where is the Risk in the Desktop Outsourcing project?

1024. How many more potential communications channels were introduced by the discovery of the new stakeholders?

1025. Is there adequate validation on required fields?

4.1 Project Performance Report: Desktop Outsourcing

1026. What degree are the relative importance and priority of the goals clear to all team members?

1027. To what degree does the informal organization make use of individual resources and meet individual needs?

1028. To what degree can team members vigorously define the teams purpose in considerations with others who are not part of the functioning team?

1029. To what degree are the goals ambitious?

1030. To what degree does the teams approach to its work allow for modification and improvement over time?

1031. To what degree does the teams work approach provide opportunity for members to engage in open interaction?

1032. To what degree does the teams work approach provide opportunity for members to engage in results-based evaluation?

1033. What is the degree to which rules govern information exchange between individuals within your organization?

1034. To what degree are the tasks requirements

reflected in the flow and storage of information?

1035. How can Desktop Outsourcing project sustainability be maintained?

1036. To what degree do team members agree with the goals, relative importance, and the ways in which achievement will be measured?

1037. To what degree does the information network communicate information relevant to the task?

1038. To what degree do the relationships of the informal organization motivate taskrelevant behavior and facilitate task completion?

1039. To what degree do team members understand one anothers roles and skills?

1040. To what degree are the structures of the formal organization consistent with the behaviors in the informal organization?

1041. To what degree is the information network consistent with the structure of the formal organization?

4.2 Variance Analysis: Desktop Outsourcing

1042. How does your organization measure performance?

1043. Does the contractors system identify work accomplishment against the schedule plan?

1044. Is all contract work included in the CWBS?

1045. How do you evaluate the impact of schedule changes, work around, et?

1046. Did your organization lose existing customers and/or gain new customers?

1047. What can be the cause of an increase in costs?

1048. Are the requirements for all items of overhead established by rational, traceable processes?

1049. Do you identify potential or actual budget-based and time-based schedule variances?

1050. Are material costs reported within the same period as that in which BCWP is earned for that material?

1051. What business event causes fluctuations?

1052. Does the scheduling system identify in a timely manner the status of work?

1053. Are there externalities from having some customers, even if they are unprofitable in the short run?

1054. How are variances affected by multiple material and labor categories?

1055. Who are responsible for overhead performance control of related costs?

1056. What is the incurrence of actual indirect costs in excess of budgets, by element of expense?

1057. Are there quarterly budgets with quarterly performance comparisons?

1058. Are indirect costs accumulated for comparison with the corresponding budgets?

1059. What types of services and expense are shared between business segments?

1060. Are work packages assigned to performing organizations?

4.3 Earned Value Status: Desktop Outsourcing

1061. Validation is a process of ensuring that the developed system will actually achieve the stakeholders desired outcomes; Are you building the right product? What do you validate?

1062. Where are your problem areas?

1063. Are you hitting your Desktop Outsourcing projects targets?

1064. Earned value can be used in almost any Desktop Outsourcing project situation and in almost any Desktop Outsourcing project environment. it may be used on large Desktop Outsourcing projects, medium sized Desktop Outsourcing projects, tiny Desktop Outsourcing projects (in cut-down form), complex and simple Desktop Outsourcing projects and in any market sector. some people, of course, know all about earned value, they have used it for years - but perhaps not as effectively as they could have?

1065. How does this compare with other Desktop Outsourcing projects?

1066. If earned value management (EVM) is so good in determining the true status of a Desktop Outsourcing project and Desktop Outsourcing project its completion, why is it that hardly any one uses it in information systems related Desktop Outsourcing projects?

1067. Verification is a process of ensuring that the developed system satisfies the stakeholders agreements and specifications; Are you building the product right? What do you verify?

1068. Where is evidence-based earned value in your organization reported?

1069. What is the unit of forecast value?

1070. When is it going to finish?

1071. How much is it going to cost by the finish?

4.4 Risk Audit: Desktop Outsourcing

1072. What are the strategic implications with clients when auditors focus audit resources based on business-level risks?

1073. Does your board meet regularly and document all decisions and actions?

1074. Has risk management been considered when planning an event?

1075. For this risk .. what do you need to stop doing, start doing and keep doing?

1076. Are all participants informed of safety issues?

1077. Does your organization communicate regularly and effectively with its members?

1078. To what extent are auditors effective at linking business risks and management assertions?

1079. Are procedures developed to respond to foreseeable emergencies and communicated to all involved?

1080. Tradeoff: how much risk can be tolerated and still deliver the products where they need to be?

1081. Are risk assessments documented?

1082. Is Desktop Outsourcing project scope stable?

1083. Are the best people available?

1084. How effective are your risk controls?

1085. What are the risks that could stop you from achieving your KPIs?

1086. Has an event time line been developed?

1087. Do you have an understanding of insurance claims processes?

1088. Do you have a mechanism for managing change?

1089. Do you have position descriptions for all key paid and volunteer positions in your organization?

1090. What can you do to manage outcomes?

1091. Are policies communicated to all affected?

4.5 Contractor Status Report: Desktop Outsourcing

1092. What are the minimum and optimal bandwidth requirements for the proposed solution?

1093. What was the budget or estimated cost for your organizations services?

1094. What was the overall budget or estimated cost?

1095. Describe how often regular updates are made to the proposed solution. Are corresponding regular updates included in the standard maintenance plan?

1096. What process manages the contracts?

1097. How long have you been using the services?

1098. What was the actual budget or estimated cost for your organizations services?

1099. If applicable; describe your standard schedule for new software version releases. Are new software version releases included in the standard maintenance plan?

1100. How does the proposed individual meet each requirement?

1101. Who can list a Desktop Outsourcing project as organization experience, your organization or a previous employee of your organization?

1102. How is risk transferred?

1103. What was the final actual cost?

1104. What is the average response time for answering a support call?

1105. Are there contractual transfer concerns?

4.6 Formal Acceptance: Desktop Outsourcing

1106. Who would use it?

1107. Do you perform formal acceptance or burn-in tests?

1108. Does it do what client said it would?

1109. What lessons were learned about your Desktop Outsourcing project management methodology?

1110. What can you do better next time?

1111. Was the Desktop Outsourcing project work done on time, within budget, and according to specification?

1112. Was business value realized?

1113. Do you buy pre-configured systems or build your own configuration?

1114. What is the Acceptance Management Process?

1115. Who supplies data?

1116. Was the client satisfied with the Desktop Outsourcing project results?

1117. What was done right?

1118. Was the Desktop Outsourcing project managed well?

1119. General estimate of the costs and times to complete the Desktop Outsourcing project?

1120. Does it do what Desktop Outsourcing project team said it would?

1121. What features, practices, and processes proved to be strengths or weaknesses?

1122. What are the requirements against which to test, Who will execute?

1123. How well did the team follow the methodology?

1124. Was the Desktop Outsourcing project goal achieved?

1125. Do you buy-in installation services?

5.0 Closing Process Group: Desktop Outsourcing

1126. How well defined and documented were the Desktop Outsourcing project management processes you chose to use?

1127. Can the lesson learned be replicated?

1128. What is the Desktop Outsourcing project name and date of completion?

1129. Is the Desktop Outsourcing project funded?

1130. Just how important is your work to the overall success of the Desktop Outsourcing project?

1131. What were the desired outcomes?

1132. What areas does the group agree are the biggest success on the Desktop Outsourcing project?

1133. What is an Encumbrance?

1134. How critical is the Desktop Outsourcing project success to the success of your organization?

1135. Is this a follow-on to a previous Desktop Outsourcing project?

1136. How will you know you did it?

1137. Did the Desktop Outsourcing project team have

enough people to execute the Desktop Outsourcing project plan?

1138. Is the Desktop Outsourcing project funded?

1139. What could have been improved?

1140. Did the Desktop Outsourcing project team have the right skills?

1141. Were the outcomes different from the already stated planned?

5.1 Procurement Audit: Desktop Outsourcing

1142. Is the purchasing department organizationally independent of the departments using that function?

1143. Is free and fair (international) competition promoted by organizational policies and legislation, in line with legal, trade organizations and other policies?

1144. Is sufficient evidence required for all disbursements (except nominal amounts)?

1145. Is it clear which procurement procedure your organization has opted for?

1146. Was the award criteria that of the most economically advantageous tender?

1147. Are advantages and disadvantages of in-house production, outsourcing and Public Private Partnerships considered?

1148. Is a risk evaluation performed?

1149. Do at least two people have custodial responsibilities for negotiable checks (one checking on the other)?

1150. Are the responsibilities of the purchasing department clearly defined?

1151. Are travel expenditures monitored to determine that they are in line with other employees and reasonable for the area of travel?

1152. Who had not previously applied to participate?

1153. Does your organization make sources of information beyond the tender documents equally available for all the candidates?

1154. Is there management monitoring of transactions and balances?

1155. Does procurement staff have skills to procure complex or special items (i.e. IT)?

1156. Are required quality and service standards set?

1157. Are obtained prices/qualities competitive to prices/qualities obtained by other procurement functions/units, comparing obtained or improved value for money?

1158. Were additional works charged at the unit prices agreed in the initial contract?

1159. Are the responsibilities for monitoring the execution and performance of contracts clearly assigned?

1160. Was the estimated contract value in line with the final cost of the contract awarded?

1161. Is the chosen supplier part of your organizations database?

5.2 Contract Close-Out: Desktop Outsourcing

1162. Was the contract complete without requiring numerous changes and revisions?

1163. Have all contract records been included in the Desktop Outsourcing project archives?

1164. Was the contract sufficiently clear so as not to result in numerous disputes and misunderstandings?

1165. Parties: who is involved?

1166. Have all contracts been closed?

1167. Change in circumstances?

1168. Change in knowledge?

1169. Change in attitude or behavior?

1170. Parties: Authorized?

1171. Why Outsource?

1172. Has each contract been audited to verify acceptance and delivery?

1173. What happens to the recipient of services?

1174. What is capture management?

1175. Was the contract type appropriate?

1176. How/when used ?

1177. Have all acceptance criteria been met prior to final payment to contractors?

1178. Have all contracts been completed?

1179. How does it work?

1180. How is the contracting office notified of the automatic contract close-out?

1181. Are the signers the authorized officials?

5.3 Project or Phase Close-Out: Desktop Outsourcing

1182. Who controlled the resources for the Desktop Outsourcing project?

1183. Did the delivered product meet the specified requirements and goals of the Desktop Outsourcing project?

1184. Were cost budgets met?

1185. Who exerted influence that has positively affected or negatively impacted the Desktop Outsourcing project?

1186. What could be done to improve the process?

1187. What are the marketing communication needs for each stakeholder?

1188. What were the goals and objectives of the communications strategy for the Desktop Outsourcing project?

1189. In addition to assessing whether the Desktop Outsourcing project was successful, it is equally critical to analyze why it was or was not fully successful. Are you including this?

1190. How much influence did the stakeholder have over others?

1191. Planned remaining costs?

1192. Complete yes or no?

1193. In preparing the Lessons Learned report, should it reflect a consensus viewpoint, or should the report reflect the different individual viewpoints?

1194. How often did each stakeholder need an update?

1195. Who controlled key decisions that were made?

1196. Was the schedule met?

1197. Is the lesson significant, valid, and applicable?

1198. Was the user/client satisfied with the end product?

1199. What is this stakeholder expecting?

5.4 Lessons Learned: Desktop Outsourcing

1200. How closely did deliverables match what was defined within the Desktop Outsourcing project Scope?

1201. How useful and complete was the Desktop Outsourcing project document repository?

1202. How often do communications get lost?

1203. Did the delivered product meet the specified requirements and goals of the Desktop Outsourcing project?

1204. What is the distribution of authority?

1205. How well is the build process working?

1206. How much of your time was spent on other than this Desktop Outsourcing project?

1207. What things surprised you on the Desktop Outsourcing project that were not in the plan?

1208. Were any strategies or activities unsuccessful?

1209. How well were your expectations met regarding the extent of your involvement in the Desktop Outsourcing project (effort, time commitments, etc.)?

1210. What was the single greatest success and the

single greatest shortcoming or challenge from the Desktop Outsourcing projects perspective?

1211. Recommendation: what do you recommend should be done to ensure that others throughout your organization can benefit from what you have learned?

1212. Was the necessary hardware, software, accommodation etc available?

1213. How smooth do you feel Integration has been?

1214. Do you have any real problems?

1215. What are the external dependencies?

1216. What report generation capability is needed?

1217. What is the skill mix defined for the staffing?

1218. Do you conduct the engineering tests?

1219. Did the Desktop Outsourcing project change significantly?

Index

addressed   136, 165, 197, 225, 237
addressing   42
adequate   37, 138, 147-148, 194, 240
adequately   33, 209, 226, 228
adjust 91, 96
adjusted   93
adjusting   138
advance   152, 210, 230
advancing   225
advantage   59, 106, 185
advantages   122, 161, 255
adverse   189
affect 66, 68, 71, 114, 121, 135, 144, 146, 199, 221-222
affected   133, 195, 207-208, 213, 244, 248, 259
affecting   11, 18, 61, 135
affective   236
affordable   89
against34, 93, 100, 202, 211, 236, 243, 252
agencies   203
agenda   230
agendas   106
agents 183
aggregate   51
agreed   207-208, 256
agreement   5, 104, 138, 141, 230-231
agreements   68, 87, 246
aiming 117
alerts   101
aligned   21
Alignment   207
alleged   1
alliance   86
allocate   124
allocated   48, 53
allocating   153, 190
allocation   153
allowable   48
allowed   124, 167
allows 9
almost 245
already   117, 152, 186, 218, 254
always 9
ambiguous   232

287

present   96, 105, 107, 141, 175, 203, 207, 213
presented   25, 229
preserve   31
preserved   71
pressing   127
prevailing   201
prevent   46, 138, 152, 199, 225
prevents   23
previous   39, 162, 249, 253
previously   139, 197, 221, 256
prices 256
primary   53
priorities   50-51, 55, 182
priority 44, 55, 160, 241
privacy   137
Private 135, 255
probable   203
probably   167
problem   15, 17-19, 22, 24-27, 32, 35, 39, 52-53, 59, 65, 143,
217, 223, 245
problems   15, 18, 21, 76, 85, 89, 97, 143, 186-187, 262
procedural   236
procedure   255
procedures   9, 93, 99-101, 138, 152, 155-156, 165, 170, 176-
177, 181, 183, 187-188, 219, 224, 231, 247
proceeding   172, 194
process   1-7, 9, 29-32, 34, 37-38, 53, 59-69, 71-72, 83, 86,
91-97, 99, 102, 127, 130, 134, 139-141, 144-149, 156, 166, 171,
177, 183, 187-188, 193-194, 201, 203-204, 211, 215, 223, 228, 235,
239, 245-246, 249, 251, 253, 259, 261
processes   45, 56, 58-66, 68, 71, 95-96, 101, 127, 134-135,
170, 184, 198, 222, 226, 231, 243, 248, 252-253
procure   256
procuring   216
produce   69, 129, 135, 165, 178, 217, 228
produced   72, 87, 147
produces   159
producing   144
product   1, 56, 67, 121-122, 130, 141, 146, 184-185, 200,
205, 217-218, 221, 228, 237, 245-246, 259-261
production   33, 88, 105, 231, 255
products   1, 15, 24, 56, 109, 113, 130, 134-135, 140, 144,
182, 216, 218, 247

CPSIA information can be obtained
at www.ICGtesting.com
Printed in the USA
BVHW082023110819
555624BV00016BA/1665/P